W9-BXY-206

CURLING, ETCETERA

CURLING, ETCETERA
A Whole Bunch of Stuff about the Roaring Game

BOB WEEKS

John Wiley & Sons Canada, Ltd.

Library and Archives Canada Cataloguing in Publication Data

Weeks, Bob
    Curling, etcetera : a whole bunch of stuff about the roaring game / Bob Weeks.

Includes index.
ISBN 978-0-470-15613-1

    1. Curling. I. Title.
GV845.W3858 2008   796.964   C2008-902118-5

Production Credits
Cover design: Jason Vandenberg
Interior design and typesetting: Mike Chan
Cover photo: Hulton Archive/Getty Images
Printer: Tri-graphic Printing

John Wiley & Sons Canada, Ltd.
6045 Freemont Blvd.
Mississauga, Ontario
L5R 4J3

Printed in Canada

1 2 3 4 5 TRI 12 11 10 09 08

This book is printed with biodegradable vegetable-based inks. Text pages are printed on 60lb. 100% PCW recycled paper.

FSC
Mixed Sources
Product group from well-managed
forests, controlled sources and
recycled wood or fiber
Cert no. SW-COC-001352
www.fsc.org
© 1996 Forest Stewardship Council

To Peter, Alfie and Ken——the guys who opened the door for me

ACKNOWLEDGEMENTS

This book exists because I have a strange capacity for remembering all sorts of useless bits of information. Well, useless may be too strong a word, but certainly unusual and offbeat. Over the many years that I've written about curling and covered curling events, I've always managed to store in my mind not only the winners and losers but small associated items that wouldn't make the main column. I never had a place to put all these items . . . until now.

This book is a collection of years of these tidbits, the sum of which I hope will intrigue you. However, as sharp as I believed my memory was, I was still a bit foggy on certain facts and needed verification from a number of sources. Chief among these was Warren Hansen, the Canadian Curling Association's director of competitions. He knows as much about curling as anyone and—once again—graciously passed on a correction or clarification of certain events. If there's someone who has done more for curling in this world, I've yet to meet them.

Many others pitched in as well: Jeff Timson, Keith Wendorf, John Kawaja, Danny Lamoureux, George Karrys, and the late Doug Maxwell were the primary aids.

I also couldn't have managed this project without the assistance of my co-publishers of the *Ontario Curling Report*: Peter Birchard, Alfie Phillips Jr., and Ken Thompson. They are three wonderful guys who have as much passion for the game as they do for red wine.

There is a shrinking but still strong fraternity of curling media who also pitched in (whether they knew it or not): Alan Cameron, Paul Wiecek, Jim Bender, Bob Garvin, Jim "Hollywood" Henderson, Brian McAndrew, Bill Graveland, Terry Jones, Vicki Hall, Mike Burns Jr., and the web-heads Dallas Bittle and Gerry Guerts.

Many of the game's best players also answered questions for me either in person, on the phone, or via e-mail. Thanks to Russ Howard, Glenn Howard, Richard Hart, Dave Nedohin, Mike Harris, Ed Werenich, Kevin Martin, Joan McCusker, Hans Frauenlob, and Randy Ferbey. A special acknowledgment to Paul Savage, who may have enjoyed the game more than anyone I know.

The gang over at Wiley continue to amaze me with their talent and enthusiasm. Karen Milner had the faith to give this project the go-ahead and led a team that has shown a lot of faith in the roaring game.

Finally, to my family. My parents, Bill and Deane, are my biggest fans and the feeling is mutual. My sister, Carol, is simply the most remarkable person I've ever met. Her husband, Dennis, is a close second. And my son, Chris, I am so proud to be your father. You are the centre of my universe.

Bob Weeks
May 2008

WHAT'S IN A NAME?

Curling did not get its name because the rocks arc as they travel down the ice. That's known because the sport was called curling long before there was any intentional turn applied to the stone. The name "curling" is believed to come from an old Scottish word, "curr," which refers to the roaring sound the stones made as they slid over the frozen lochs.

In-turns and out-turns came much later. In the book *The History of Curling* by Reverend John Kerr, published in 1890, the author details what was called the Twist:

> "…to be able by a turn of the wrist to give the stone a rotary motion which shall make it run against the bias of the ice, or to transform an object of offence into one of defence by making the stone curve round the right or left side of a guard by an elbow-out or an elbow-in delivery, is one of the highest accomplishments in the art of curling and greatly increases the interest and skill of the player."

Kerr also referred to this type of shot as the Fenwick Twist because it was a group of curlers from a village of the same name who were the first to purposely utilize this type of shot.

THE HARMONICA MAN

Piping the players onto the ice before draws of major championships is standard practice these days, but it wasn't always so. At the first few Briers, held inside Toronto's Granite Club, the curlers were actually paraded onto the ice surface by a man playing a harmonica. Art Condie, who was one of the early directors of the Brier, would play his harmonica at both the opening and closing ceremonies of the competition, usually leading the curlers to the ice. In 1940, when the Brier moved into an arena in Winnipeg, Condie's harmonica was simply too quiet to be heard by the fans. Still, he was allowed to perform at the closing ceremonies and was listed in the program as the Official Brier Musician.

CLUB OF CHAMPIONS

The Strathcona Curling Club in Winnipeg, Manitoba, holds the distinction of being the home club for the most Brier-winning teams. It has seven Canadian championships to its credit.

STOP, START, THEN STOP AGAIN

It's not often someone retires, then un-retires only to retire all without playing a game. United States skip Bruce Roberts, however, did just that in 1984. Roberts was a three-time U.S. men's champion, winning in 1967, '76 and '77, also taking the 1976 World Championship. But after that run, the resident of Duluth, Minnesota, retired from competitive curling, in part due to injuries.

But the 1984 World Championship was hosted in Duluth, and Roberts decided he wanted to make one more try at the Silver Broom in front of his hometown fans. And so, with his brother Joe throwing last rocks, he made a comeback and played exceptionally well, losing just four competitive games all year en route to representing the U.S.A. at the world final.

Despite the success, Roberts stated prior to the start of his comeback year that he would be retiring when the season was over. So, effectively, he announced his un-retirement and re-retirement all at the same time.

Roberts and his American rink lost a final round-robin game to Germany to finish with a 5–4 mark, one game short of the playoffs. True to his word, the U.S. Curling Hall of Famer hung up his broom—again—at the end of the '84 World Championship.

CITY ACCESS

For five years, two cities were given entry into the Brier. Teams representing Montreal and Toronto fielded rinks in the Canadian men's national championship from 1927 to 1931 before being dropped in favour of provincial entries only. In 43 games, the Montreal team won just 10 matches. Toronto's team played 46 games—including three playoff contests—and came out on top in 28 of those.

AMERICAN SUCCESS

The Bemidji Curling Club in Bemidji, Minnesota, is easily one of the most successful in the United States, if not the world. The club can lay claim to having 18 U.S. national championship teams and 50 state championship rinks, a record that most clubs can only envy.

DEBBIE MCCORMICK

One of the most successful curlers in U.S. history, Debbie McCormick played in five World Junior Championships, six World Curling Championships, and two Olympics. A few notes on the American curler:

- She is the only American woman to skip a team to the World Championship title.
- Her World Championship title in 2003 was the first time she skipped in international play.
- She was born in Saskatoon, Saskatchewan, but moved to Madison, Wisconsin, when very young, when her father was transferred there for business.
- She posed nude for a calendar created to promote women's curling.
- She won the U.S. national title four times.
- Her father, Wally, played in two World Championships, finishing third both times.
- Her good-luck charm is a ticket from the gold-medal women's curling game at the 1998 Olympics, autographed by the members of the winning Sandra Schmirler team.

CURLING IN PRINT

One of the earliest mentions of curling in print is found in Thomas Pennant's book *Tour Through Scotland*, published in 1772. He describes the game as follows:

"Of all the sports in those parts, that of curling is the favorite. It is an amusement of the winter, and played upon the ice, by sliding from one mark to another, great stones of 40 to 70 lbs weight, of a hemispherical form, with a wooden or iron handle on top. The object of the player is to lay his stone as near the mark as possible, to guard that of his partner which has been well laid before, or to strike off that of his antagonist."

MOTOR CITY, CANADA

Cross-border curling: The Detroit Curling Club is a member of the Ontario Curling Association.

STONE STANDARD

For many years, curling stones came in all sorts of shapes and sizes. While there was an attempt made to somewhat standardize the stones over time, in the early 1800s the Grand Caledonian Curling Club came up with a scale for the ratio of diameter to thickness, shown below. Prior to this scale, rocks were often twice as wide as they were thick.

The Scale
When the weight of the stone is under the maximum height not to be more than

35 lbs.	4.25 inches
38 lbs.	4.5 inches
41 lbs.	4.75 inches
44 lbs.	5 inches
47 lbs.	5.25 inches
50 lbs.	5.5 inches

"Whatever the diameter or weight, the height ought never to exceed 6⅛ inches, nor be less than 4¼ inches. None [ought] to be allowed in a set game of greater diameter than 12 inches, nor of a greater weight than 50 lbs. Imperial."

THE 12 RULES OF CURLING

When the Toronto Curling Club began play in Canada's largest centre, it did so on the frozen shoreline of Lake Ontario. The club was originally made up mostly of transplanted Scots who came from a variety of villages in the homeland and, as a result, had a variety of rules owing to the changes from village to village. So one of the first tasks of the new group was to craft an original set of Rules of the Game, which they did in about 1840. There were just 12 "laws" set out for play, some of which are still in use today:

1. The rink to be forty-two yards from tee to tee, unless otherwise agreed upon by the parties. When a game is begun the rink cannot be changed or altered unless by the consent of a majority of players, and it can be shortened only when it is apparent that a majority cannot play the length.

2. The hog score must be distant from the tee one-sixth part of the length of the rink. Every stone to be deemed a hog, the sole of which, when at rest, does not completely clear the length.

3. Every player to foot so that in delivering his stone, it shall pass over the tee.

4. The order of playing adopted at the beginning must not be changed during a game.

5. Curling stones must be of a circular shape. No stone to be changed during a game unless it happens to be broken; and the largest fragment of such stone to count, without any necessity of playing it more. If a stone roll or be upset, it must be placed on its sole where it stops. Should the handle quit a stone in delivery, the player must keep hold of it, otherwise he will not be entitled to replay the shot.

6. The player may sweep his own stone the whole length of the rink; his party not to sweep until it has passed the first hog score, and his adversaries not to sweep until it has passed the tee—the sweeping to be always to a side.

7. None of the players, on any account, to cross or go upon the middle of the rink.

8. If, in sweeping or otherwise, a running stone is marred by any of the party to which it belongs, it must be put off the rink; if by any of the adverse party, it must be placed agreeably to the direction which was given to the player; and if it be marred by any other means, the player may take his shot again. Should a stone at rest be accidentally displaced, it must be put as near as possible in its former situation.

9. Every player must be ready when his turn comes and must take only a reasonable time to play his shot. Should he, by mistake, play a wrong stone, it must be replaced wherever it stops, by the one which he ought to have played.

10. A doubtful shot must be measured by a neutral per-

son, whose determination shall be final.

11. The skip alone shall direct the game. The players of the respective skips may offer them their advice, but cannot control their directions; nor is any person except the skip to address him who is about to play. Each skip may appoint one of his party to take the charge for him, when he is about to play.

Every player to follow the direction given to him.

12. Should any question arise, the determination of which may not be provided for by the words and spirit of the preceding Rules, each party to choose one of their number in order to determine it. If the two so chosen differ in their opinion, they are to name an umpire whose decision shall be final.

Curling Quote

"We can't bring him in, he spilled red wine all over his uniform."

—Richard Hart to skip Mike Harris during the 1997 Canadian curling trials. The team's second, Colin Mitchell, was hurt, and Harris wanted to bring in the team's fifth player/coach and noted bon vivant, Paul Savage, to fill in. The clip was heard across the TSN broadcast of the event.

SAY WHAT?

Many of the terms used in the early days of curling have disappeared from the game's lexicon. Here are a few that used to be quite common in the late 1700s and early 1800s.

Term	Meaning
Break an egg on	To strike one stone very gently with another
Brough	The House
Chuckle to	To rub off the inside of two or more guards en route to another stone.
Director	The Skip
Hindhand	The player who throws the last rock on his team, usually the skip
Lie in the bosom of	To freeze to another rock
Redd the ice	to clear guards from the front of the rings

BURNS ON CURLING

The great poet Robert Burns may not have been a champion curler, but he did mention the grand old game in his poem "Tam Samson's Elegy." The fourth verse of the piece reads as follows:

> When Winter muffles up his cloak,
> And binds the mire like a rock;
> When to the loughs the curlers flock,
> Wi' gleesome speed,
> Wha will they station at the cock? -
> 'Tam Samson's dead!'

The standard English translation of that work was provided by the Robert Burns World Foundation:

> When Winter muffles up his cloak,
> And binds the mire like a rock;
> When to the ponds the curlers flock,
> With gleeful speed,
> Who will they station at the cock (mark)? -
> 'Tam Samson is dead!'

TWO TIMES EIGHT

Scoring an eight-ender—a perfect end—is an achievement ranked as one of the most difficult in sport. Many players compete their entire career without even witnessing one. But in 1993 the team of Kim Gellard, Corie Beveridge, Lisa Savage, and Sandy Graham accomplished something that had never been done before or since. Playing in a school league, the team recorded consecutive eight-enders—two perfect ends. "It's amazing," commented Gellard, the skip. No curler alive would disagree.

Curling Quote
"Blood is thicker than Screech."

—Russ Howard on why he was cheering for his brother, Glenn, over his former Newfoundland teammates, led by Brad Gushue in the 2007 Brier final

PAUL SAVAGE

Paul Savage has been around the game of curling since he was a teenager, growing up in Don Mills, Ontario, and following in the footsteps of another Ontario icon, Alf Phillips Junior. He won titles all over Canada and competed around the world, and is known as a talented and fun-loving player. A few notes about Paul Savage:

- His first provincial title was the 1965 Ontario Schoolboy, which he won while representing Don Mills Collegiate Institute.
- He appeared in the movie *Men With Brooms*, playing a minor role as a curling broadcaster, calling the action of the film's ultimate match.
- He was the fifth man on Mike Harris's Canadian Olympic team, which played in the 1998 Games in Nagano, Japan. To qualify for a medal, he was required to play at least one end. He actually played two,

in a game against Germany in which Canada had already posted a healthy lead. That allowed him to earn a silver medal. At 50, he was the oldest medalist in the '98 Games.

- Prior to leaving for the Olympics, he had the Olympic rings tattooed onto his rear end. A picture of the tattoo appeared on the front page of a Toronto newspaper.
- He played in seven Briers, winning once as third for Ed Werenich in 1983, and finishing second on three other occasions.

- After his playing career, Savage became an entrepreneur in the game, starting an Ontario-based skins game, which grew to become a nationally televised event pitting the top teams in Eastern Canada vs. those in Western Canada.
- He was on the losing end of one of the greatest comebacks in Brier history. In the 1974 Brier, he was leading Hec Gervais by seven points after six ends but lost in an extra end—the 11th.

- He was given the nickname "the Round Mound of Come Around". by the Ontario Curling Report owing to his girth as well as his talent for playing the draw shot. It was a play on the nickname of NBA player Charles Barkley, who was known as the "Round Mound of Rebound."
- Paul's daughter, Lisa, was the 1994 World Junior champion.

AMERICAN ORIGINS

The first curling club in the United States was formed in Orchard Lake, Michigan, in 1831, six years before the state officially joined the union that would become the United States of America.

MOVING INDOORS
IN THE U.S.A.

Although curling was a popular sport in the United States at the turn of the century, it was rarely played indoors. An exhibition match in 1897 in Brooklyn, New York, is believed to be the first time curling was played in a covered rink in America, but it wasn't until 1910 that it was first played on an indoor rink. That event took place in Boston at the Boston Arena when three sheets were put into a skating rink in order to host a bonspiel.

The first United States Men's Curling Championship, however, took that to another level with a rather impressive start. The championship was held in Chicago in 1957 at the Chicago Stadium, an 18,000-seat arena that served as home to the NHL's Chicago Black Hawks and the NBA's Chicago Bulls. It was also broadcast on regional television. The winner of that inaugural contest was a rink from Hibbing, Minnesota, skipped by Harold Lauber.

PASSPORT, PLEASE

Canadian ex-pats have taken their game to many countries over the years and represented those countries at a high level.

Here is a selection of Canadian-born skips who have represented countries other than their native land in the world championships:

Hugh Milliken

Canadian	Country Represented	Year First Represented
Bob Woods	Sweden	1967
Keith Wendorf	Germany	1978
Roger Schmidt	Germany	1987
Maymar Gemmell	USA	1991
Hugh Milliken	Australia	1992
Patti Lank	U.S.A.	1997
Dan Mustapic	New Zealand	2001

A BOY AMONG MEN

The youngest player to compete at the world championships was 15-year-old Sjur Loen, who skipped Norway's entry in 1974. At that time, there were no age restrictions, and Loen's team of Hans Bekkelund (16), Morten Sogaard (17), and Hans Okelsrud (18) managed a record of 2–7. The next year, the first World Junior Curling Championship was held in Toronto, and although Loen didn't compete in that event, he represented Norway from 1976 to 1979, with his best finish coming in 1976, when he ended third. Loen managed to make it into the men's world championship nine more times, winning it twice.

THE MEASUREMENT OF A CURLING STONE

Curlers throw rocks up and down the sheet hundreds, perhaps thousands of times in a season, but do they ever stop to consider just how wide or heavy the curling stone really is? While stones are generally consistent from club to club and rink to rink, there is some provision in the rule book for a bit of variety. Here's what the rule book dictates:

> Curling stones, including handle and bolt, shall weigh a maximum of 44 pounds (19.96 kilograms) and a minimum of 38.5 pounds (17.46 kilograms), shall have a maximum circumference of 36 inches (91.44 centimetres), and shall be a maximum of 5.5 inches (13.97 centimetres) in height, measured between the bottom and top of the stone.

The rules indicate maximums for circumference and height, and a maximum and minimum for weight, so there is room to create a shorter, narrower, and lighter rock. So far, however, most manufacturers use the maximums as the standard measurements.

THE FIRST CURLING STAR?

Howard Wood of Winnipeg was one of the first curlers to achieve notoriety across a wide swath of Canada. A three-time Brier champion, he was a vivacious, gregarious man who quickly became popular with opponents and fans. A few notes about Wood:

- He began curling in 1903 on a backyard rink built by his father.
- In 1908, he played in his first Manitoba Bonspiel, the first of what would be a remarkable 70 consecutive appearances in the grand championship. That mark put him into the *Guinness Book of World Records*. He managed to win the overall title on eight occasions.
- In 1925, Wood and his team won an all-expenses-paid trip to tour Ontario and Quebec, and curl teams in that part of the country. The rink played 19 games and won 18 of them, several by more than 20 points.
- Wood won his first Brier in 1930 playing skip. Two years later, he won again, but this time playing third for Johnny Congalton. While many players have won a Brier at lead, second, or third and then later won as a skip, dropping down in position as Wood did is a feat that wasn't matched again until Pat Ryan, who skipped the Canadian champions in 1988 and '89, won as third for Rick Folk in 1994.
- Wood's son, Howard Jr., became an accomplished curler,

and played third for his father when they won the Brier in 1940. To distinguish between the two, the senior Wood became known affectionately as Pappy.

- The 1940 Brier was the first to be played in an arena, the Winnipeg Amphitheatre. The final round was played before 5,000 fans, and they were not disappointed. Wood and his Manitoba team beat Cliff Manahan's Alberta foursome 17–11 to clinch the title.
- In 1947, Wood won the first Carspiel, a competitive event that awarded four cars as first prize. Wood had to play a delicate-weight double with his final shot to win the title. It appeared to be a shot that was next to impossible to make. But Wood threw the rock and without waiting for it to finish, calmly walked over to one of the cars that had been conveniently brought onto the ice as a marketing tool, opened the door, and sat down in the driver's seat, just in time to watch the rock make the perfect split and come to rest for a single point and the title. He and his team drove home from Nipawin, Saskatchewan, in four new Hudsons.

Curling Fact

According to the Canada Curling Stone Company, the average lifespan of a curling stone is 50 years, and it can travel up to two hundred kilometres a year, up and down a sheet of ice.

CARVED IN GRANITE

The first Canadian men's curling championship was held in 1927 at Toronto's Granite Curling Club. The event was held there continuously until 1939 and one final time in 1941. Some facts about the original home of the Brier:

- The club was started in 1875 by five prominent Toronto businessmen who were members of the Toronto Curling Club. They were unhappy at the direction of that club and its decision to build a new facility on Adelaide Street.
- The first honorary patron of the new club was Sir John A. Macdonald, Canada's first prime minister.
- The club's first site was on a parcel of land just east of Queen's Park, the provincial legislature. The land was leased and the club built for $700. In future years, the club moved to locations on Church Street, north of Wellesley, and then, in 1926, to St. Clair Avenue, just west of Yonge. Its current location is on Bayview Avenue.
- One of the main reasons to build the facility on St. Clair was to install artificial ice. In 1924 and '25, because of mild conditions, there had been almost no curling at the Church Street club, which had natural ice. When completed, the new rink was called "the largest single covered expanse of

artificial ice on the American continent."

- Curling was only one of many sports available to members of the Granite Curling Club. Tennis, golf, swimming, bowling, badminton, and skating were all part of the lineup although curling remained the primary focus for many years.

- A hockey team from the Granite Curling Club won the gold medal at the 1924 Olympics.

U.S. COLLEGIATE CURLING

While it's not quite on the same level as the Rose Bowl, there is a U.S. collegiate curling championship held annually. College curling began with the Illinois State Curling Foundation, which was established to administer a trust left by Darwin Curtis, an enthusiastic curler from Wilmette, Illinois. It started with a program to introduce college-aged curlers to the game in the mid-1980s and has grown into a true national bonspiel. In 2007, 30 teams were in the event, now held annually in Madison, Wisconsin. Among the schools that field teams are Harvard, MIT, Rutgers, and the University of Minnesota.

SIX-SHOOTER

Only once has a Brier held in an arena had more than five sheets of ice. In Hamilton in 1991, because the ice surface was built to handle international hockey (which has a wider rink than North American hockey), six sheets of ice were built on the floor of Copps Coliseum. That allowed organizers to run an event with no morning draws, the only time that's happened. In total, only 14 draws were held, and attendance reached 88,894.

Curling Quote

"I'm sure it was boring to watch. We could hear some people yelling down at us on the ice. It was frustrating for us too."

—British Columbia skip Rick Folk commenting on his 3-2 loss to Pat Ryan in the final of the 1989 Brier, regarded as one of the most uninteresting, boring Canadian finals ever

OUT OF THE COLD

The first indoor curling rink with artificial ice opened in 1907 in Crossmyloof, Scotland.

CROWDED HOUSE

Brier attendance records have been kept since 1946, although in the early days, they were little more than estimates. The highest attendance came in 2005 in Edmonton when 281,985 people watched the competition. The lowest was in 1971 in Quebec City when just 8,501 fans showed up. That's the only time since '46 that fewer than 10,000 people watched the Canadian championship, although it should be noted that a major snowstorm limited travel for much of the week.

KEN WATSON, MR. CURLING

In the 1930s and '40s, Ken Watson was known across Canada as Mr. Curling, and a look at his record shows the name was justified. Watson won three Briers as well as a host of other notable events, and was instrumental in starting the Scotch Cup, which was the forerunner of the world championships.

Here are some facts about Watson:

- He was born in 1904 in Minnedosa, Manitoba, the son of a reverend.
- He started curling at 15, and his first curling prize was a butter knife.
- He skipped the Brier-winning rink in 1939, '42, and '49.
- Many felt he would have won more Briers, but the championship was put on hold from 1943 to 1945 because of the Second World War, right at the peak of Watson's career.
- He was one of the first people to slide while delivering the rock. He accomplished this by taking off his rubber, which all curlers wore on their shoes at the time, and sliding on the sole of his shoe. In later years, he affixed solder to the bottom of his shoe so he could slide even farther. He was roundly criticized by many traditionalists for this shocking delivery.
- He wrote a best-selling book, *Ken Watson on Curling*, which listed the Seven C's for Success: Compatibility, Concentration,

Co-operation, Courage, Confidence, Competitiveness, and Consistency.

- In 1959, against the wishes of the Canadian (then Dominion) Curling Association, Watson set up matches between the Canadian champions, the Richardsons, and Willie Young and his Scottish champs. That tournament led eventually to the start of the World Curling Championship.
- For 20 years, Watson made his living as a high school teacher, but because of his notoriety, he went into the insurance business and was extremely successful.
- Watson won the overall title in the Manitoba Bonspiel, the largest event in the world, a remarkable six consecutive times, from 1942–47.

Charles Reid, Lyle Dyker, Grant Watson, and Ken Watson with their Brier trophy in 1949.

SWEEP, THEN PUSH

For many years, push brooms were used almost exclusively in Europe, while North American curlers played with corn brooms. But in the 1970s, the tide turned, and much of the impetus to switch was the result of play at one curling club. The Calgary Winter Club was one of the first facilities in Canada to offer up push brooms for club use, putting them into play in the late 1960s. Curlers at that popular rink found that the push brooms were more effective because they never left the ice surface, less taxing on the body, and far less messy. Not surprisingly, the brooms took off.

The peak of success may have been 1975, when three teams from the club won national championships—all sweeping with push brooms. The rinks won the Canadian mixed, Canadian junior boys, and the Canada Winter Games.

"They are made right in Calgary and I think they are comparable to the corn brooms in effectiveness. There are places where you can keep working with the push broom when you couldn't with a corn broom. You don't wear yourself out as much in a long playdown, and you don't get arm weary," said Les Rowland, who skipped his team to the 1975 national mixed—the first Canadian championship team to use push brooms.

WARMING UP IS RUBBISH

In most sports these days, warming up is par for the course. Players in baseball have batting practice, basketball players have a shoot-around, and hockey players skate circles prior to the puck drop. But in curling, warming up was not allowed until 1976. In major competitions such as national or world championships, even walking down the ice to the far end—as skips were required to do—had to be done at the side of the sheet. Walking down the middle of the ice before the first rock was thrown was tantamount to cheating. Sliding or sweeping on the sheet was also a breach of etiquette.

But in 1975 Warren Hansen, who was a member of the 1974 Canadian championship team, and Laurie Newton, a postgraduate student at the University of Alberta, prepared a report for the International Curling Federation (ICF, forerunner of the World Curling Federation) that showed sweeping to be "one of the most vigorous movements in sports." As well, players could "reduce strains, sprains, muscle pulls and cramps" if they were permitted to slide before the contest.

Hansen made the presentation to the ICF, and while it was generally accepted, Robin Welsh, longtime secretary of the Royal Caledonian Curling Club, wasn't in that camp. He stated: "I believe it is all a pile of rubbish, curling is a manly game."

However, the majority was on Hansen's side, and on the basis of the document, a warm-up period was permitted at the 1976 Silver Broom, the first of its kind. The warm-up did not, however, include throwing any rocks. That didn't happen until 1978, when a 10-minute warm-up was allowed; however, the players were not permitted to practise on the sheet on which they were playing. Finally in 1980, each team was permitted 10 minutes to throw stones on their own sheet.

KNOW YOUR WIDTHS

Did you know that the hog line is actually thicker than the tee line or the back line? It's true—the hog line is four inches wide, while the tee and back lines are a mere half inch. These measurements are set under the rules of the game.

ALL ABOARD

In the 1940s and '50s, before air travel, a dedicated train travelled across the country, picking up Brier competitors en route to the host site. It was known as the Brier Special and allowed the competitors to get to know each other prior to the competition. The event sponsor, Macdonald Tobacco, added a bar car that became the focal point of the ride. However, the atmosphere often took its toll on the players.

"By the time I got off the train in Moncton," said Edmonton's Matt Baldwin of his trip to the 1956 championship, "I was shaking. We'd been drinking for five straight days."

WHAT A HACK

A hack may be something many curlers take for granted, but in 1989, it underwent a revolution thanks to a Quebec curler. Marco Ferraro was a competitive curler who always had difficulty with hacks wherever he played. He felt they were inconsistent, didn't provide a good hold for the foot, and often got in the way of the delivery. "It just became a case of put up or shut up," he said.

The old-style hacks were sunk into the ice and were not ergonomically designed with the foot in mind. Ferraro's first stop was Montreal's Olympic Stadium, where he spent time examining the runners' starting blocks.

The Marco Hack

"I figured that an athlete going for a gold medal isn't going to leave anything to chance. He's only going to put his foot in something that's perfect," Ferraro noted.

He took that information to a mathematician who provided information on the exact angles of the foot during the delivery and then produced some prototypes. Those were tested by several top-ranked curlers, who made suggestions, and the final product was brought to market. These days, just about anywhere in the world there's a curling rink, you'll find one of these hacks, which are emblazoned with the name MARCO across the top.

THE JUBILEE STONE

Before standardization of stones, curling was played with implements of varying shapes, sizes, and weights. In fact, in some parts of Scotland, bigger stones were a sign of strength of the thrower. Players brought their own rocks to games, and the rocks were often plucked from rivers, which had worn them smooth. One of the most famous is known as the Jubilee Stone, which weighed in at a massive 53 kilograms (117 pounds). It was given its name when it was presented to the Royal Caledonian Curling Club at the governing body's Jubilee Meeting in 1888. It is on display at the club's headquarters in Edinburgh, Scotland.

PAPER GRANITE

George Plimpton made a career out of trying various sports at the top level and then writing about it from the viewpoint of an amateur. His most famous book in this genre was probably *Paper Lion*, in which he recounted his experiences playing quarterback for the Detroit Lions at the team's training camp. While his most notable works have been about sports such as football, baseball (he pitched to the American League team at the All-Star Game), and boxing (he sparred with Archie Moore), he once tried his hand at curling. Plimpton attended the 1976 Super Draw Curling Bonspiel. This event was a lottery that allowed winners to travel, all expenses paid, to Vernon, British Columbia, where they competed in a bonspiel playing for high-profile skips. Prior to the event, he admitted that the only brooms he had seen were in closets. However, he went out and skipped a team in three games, including his first with the members of Hec Gervais' 1974 Canadian championship team, while Gervais skipped three members of the media. Plimpton lost, and after he missed a takeout attempt during the contest he commented: "[The stone] must have lost interest."

CURLING FIGHTS

Curling is thought to be a game played by gentlemen and women, and in most cases, it is. However, there has been the occasion where the decorum has slipped and, just as in Canada's other great winter ice sport, fights have broken out. Here are a few incidents of fisticuffs on the curling sheets:

- During a club championship game in Winnipeg in the 1980s, two players decided that bodychecking should be a part of the game. Player A was sweeping his skip's stone into the house when it reached the tee line. At that point, Player B from the opposing team decided he wanted to sweep it as well, hoping to drag the rock farther back in the house. But his efforts to do so were stymied by Player A, who blocked him off, declaring, "It's *my* house." The two players battled for position, with Player B using his body to push Player A away from the stone. The result was plenty of pushing and shoving and tangled brooms. With the rock now stopped, the two players continued jostling, and then punches were finally thrown, with both players falling to the ice. The club president happened to be on the ice at the time and he raced over from Sheet 6 to break up the melee. Order was restored, and the game continued without any more punches being thrown.

- In 1976 in Sarnia, Ontario, two curlers in a local bonspiel began arguing when one accused the other of not releasing the stone before crossing the hog line. The argument became so intense, the player who allegedly committed the foul left the ice with his team, forfeiting the game. However, the squabble continued in the club after that and resulted in the accuser throwing a knockout punch to the head of the rock thrower. Charges were laid, and the accuser ended up in court. "Surely we aren't going to get into violence in curling," said Sarnia Judge Alan Fowler, before fining the man $250 or 25 days in jail.

- In 1982 the president of the Ottawa Curling Club sent a letter of reprimand to a member for a certain indiscretion. The member was quite upset about receiving the letter and disagreed with its accusations. During one evening's curling, the president and the member in question were playing, when the member dropped his broom, went across three sheets of ice, and clocked the president, who fell to the ice. The member received another letter, this one telling him he was banned from the club for one year. That prevented him from attending the closing men's banquet, so the member sat on a lawn chair in the parking lot of an adjoining property and threw stones at the window of the lounge where his team was eating. His teammates brought him a beer so he could at least experience a small part of the evening.

- One night at the Bobcaygeon Curling Club, Player A was celebrating his birthday prior to taking to the ice for his game. He had been knocking back the drinks, and by the time the game started, he was feeling no pain. During the game, his behaviour bothered his opposing skip, Player B, who finally confronted him, pushing his finger into his chest. The two players began pushing each other, and Player A started throwing punches, landing a few, but also slipping to the ice. Another curler ran over, grabbed the birthday boy, and put him in a headlock, keeping him that way until he tossed him out the front door of the club. The incident appeared over, but about an hour later, Player A re-appeared through the front door and challenged Player B to a fight in the parking lot. The police were called, and the Player A was removed from the property.

CURLING CLUB CHAIN GANG

When the curlers at one New York curling club throw rocks, they may not realize that their club was partially built by convicts from the state penitentiary. In 1996, the Utica Curling Club installed a new floor on which the ice for the curling club would rest. The construction crew was made up of cons who were paid 15 cents an hour for their efforts. The work program was put in place as a way to help rehabilitate the inmates. While they may not have realized it, they were supervised by one of the game's top icemakers, Dave Merklinger.

CURLING IN THE MOVIES

Help!

In the movie *Help!*, the Beatles showed they knew a little bit about the roaring game. During a winter scene, George, Paul, John, and Ringo all take part in an outdoor bonspiel—or that's what it appears is happening. George throws a rock while John and Ringo try to catch up to it and sweep. Paul is sweeping, but nowhere near the rock.

The movie's villain, Algernon, then plants a bomb in a rock and slides it down the ice toward the four musicians. Ringo sweeps the stone, which is smoking at this point. The other three realize what is in the stone, grab Ringo, and run away. Algernon, who expected the rock to explode before the boys exited, goes to check on his bomb and arrives just as it explodes.

Men with Brooms

The only feature film ever made that used curling as an underlying theme was *Men with Brooms*, starring Paul Gross of *Due South* fame. A few facts about the movie:

- The title came from a meeting between Gross and Alliance Atlantis head Robert Lantos. When Gross told him he wanted to make a truly Canadian movie and use curling as the central theme, Lantos said: "You mean that sport that has men with brooms?"

- The movie about curling drew some unusual reactions. In November 1999, Gross told the *Toronto Sun*: "When I was in Los Angeles recently, I told people I was doing this thing about curling. It was as though I had farted. They didn't know where to look."
- A number of top curlers were given cameos in the movie, including two-time Canadian champion Jeff Stoughton as well as 1983 world champion Paul Savage, who played the role of the television announcer.
- Paul Gross didn't know how to curl prior to his on-screen debut and said he used the book *Curling For Dummies* as his bible during the filming.
- Members of the rock group The Tragically Hip appeared as a curling team, representing Kingston, Ontario, their hometown.
- James Alodi, who played Neil Bucyk, one of the members of the team at the centre of the movie, fell and injured both elbows during the movie's filming. His injury, bone chips, hurt so much he wasn't able to rest his elbows on a table for weeks.
- The film opened on March 8, 2002, and set a Canadian record for opening weekend sales, with more than $1.1 million brought in at the box office. The movie opened on 213 screens. In the United States, however, it opened in September 2002 on a grand total of just 27 screens and brought in $14,765.
- A number of curling errors show up in the movie. For one, the scoreboard rarely reflects the scoring as shown on the ice.
- The budget for the movie was estimated at $7.5 million, quite small for a feature film.

NAME THAT CORN

Although they're not even made any more, corn brooms once ruled the ice, at least in North America. It wasn't until the 1970s that push brooms took over as the dominant choice for curlers of all levels. Over the years, many brooms came and went. Here are the names of a few of the more popular corn brooms of years gone by:

Rockmaster x-11
Zebra
Little Beaver
Little Otter
Little Mink
Mississauga Rattler
Pro Polka Dot
Wildcat
Thunder
8-Ender
Whipper Snapper

THE KING OF SWING

Shorty Jenkins is well-known as the first truly great icemaker in curling. Over the years he has established many techniques for making the playing surface better, and in the process he has become a well-recognized figure at major curling events. Here are some facts about the man:

- His first name is really Clarence.
- He was raised in an orphanage in Victoria, British Columbia.
- He served in the Canadian Air Force.
- He competed in the 1974 Ontario men's curling championships and experienced such bad playing conditions, he decided he would do something about it and started a career as an icemaker.
- He was the first person to time how long it took rocks to travel down the ice. He used his method to judge the condition of his surface, but it has become a much-used way of determining the changing speed of the ice by competitive teams.

- He used an infrared gun to determine the temperature of the ice and learned that different colour rock handles can absorb different amounts of heat, which can affect their speed.
- He starred in his own Tim Hortons television commercial, which was later spoofed by the Canadian comedy show *This Hour Has 22 Minutes*.
- He is often seen at curling events wearing his trademark pink cowboy hat.

WHAT IF MY ROCK...

When it comes to stones, the rule book makes provision for unusual happenings in a game. For instance, although it's rare these days for stones to break—even with the tremendous force with which they are thrown by some of the top players—Rule 4 (2) covers just that situation. It reads as follows:

> "If a stone is broken in play, a replacement stone shall be placed where the largest fragment comes to rest. The inside edge of the replacement stone shall be placed in the same position as the inside edge of the largest fragment with the assistance of a measuring stick."

If the stone doesn't break but merely flips over or comes to rest on its side, the rule book takes care of that situation in 4 (6): "A stone that rolls over in its course or comes to rest on its side or top shall be removed immediately from play."

So it seems it's better to have your rock break than flip over.

ENFANT TERRIBLE

In the 1970s and early '80s, Paul Gowsell gained a reputation for being curling's *enfant terrible*, shocking curling audiences big and small with his outlandish appearance as well as his exceptional talent. Although most of his success came as a junior and he never reached the heights some had predicted for him, tales of his antics are still told frequently in curling circles. A few stories about Paul Gowsell:

- On his way home from being honoured as Athlete of the Year in Calgary in 1977, Gowsell was stopped by police and charged with possession of marijuana.
- Gowsell was extremely nervous between games. He would often eat at the opening banquet or Calcutta (a form of betting where the teams are auctioned off, usually held at a party) on the first night and then not again until the event was over.
- Gowsell's team was the first high-profile Canadian rink to use push brooms, and it is generally credited with starting the nationwide move away from corn brooms.
- At the 1976 World Junior Championships, Gowsell was turned away from a banquet because he wasn't wearing a jacket or tie. He went back to his hotel room, put on the appropriate clothes, but returned without shoes or socks.

- At the closing banquet for the 1978 World Junior Championship, which Gowsell won, he was refused entry by a security guard who told him, "This is a banquet for curlers, not hippies."
- Gowsell was cut from his high school team in Grade 10 and 11. The following year he made the team and promptly won the Canadian junior title.
- At a major bonspiel in Winnipeg, Gowsell arranged for a pizza to be delivered to him in the middle of a game. As 1,000 fans looked on, the delivery guy walked down the sheet, handed the box to Gowsell, and took his payment. Gowsell opened the box and asked his opposing number, Larry McGrath, if he wanted a slice.

DEAD HEAT

Want to win a mug of your favourite beverage from your curling friend? Here's a trivia question that might just do the trick: Can you name two occasions when, at the conclusion of an end, there are rocks in the house but no team scores?

The answer can be found in *The Rules of Curling,* which is published by the Canadian Curling Association. The first occurs when two stones finish exactly the same distance from the centre. Under Rule 13 (8), if, after using a measuring stick, it can't be determined which of the stones is closer to the centre, then the end shall be declared blank. That is, of course, if there are no other rocks closer to the centre than the ones being measured.

The second situation happens when two rocks are so close to the centre that the measure can't be used, and it can't be determined visually which is closer. That would happen if two stones finished almost on top of the exact centre of the house.

Curling Quote

"There's nobody out here that concerns me."

—Randy Ferbey, when asked his opinion on the field at the 2005 world championship

THE ICE KING

At curling clubs around the world, a strange-looking machine is often seen preparing the surface for play, either by knee-sliding novices or world champions. The Ice King is a device that scrapes a fine layer off the top of the ice, levelling the surface and allowing a new layer of pebble to be applied. Before the invention of this motorized device, ice had to be scraped by hand, a laborious task, to be sure. A brief history of the Ice King:

- The machine was invented by Harry Mather of London, Ontario, in the mid-1960s. Mather used it at his own club. It was essentially a long blade, about half the width of a curling sheet, anchored on a plow-like device that was powered electrically. The blade could be raised or lowered depending on how much ice needed to be shaved off.
- By 1968, he'd convinced a few area clubs to buy machines that would help improve the conditions. Word spread quickly throughout Ontario, and Ice King became a viable company, selling machines.
- By the mid-1970s, Ice King was selling machines across Canada and had made some improvements to the machine, mostly cosmetic.
- In 1986, Larry Mayo and Fred Veale purchased the company from Mather and looked to improve the popular machine.

- In 1993, Bill Wood made a simple improvement by changing the power source to a battery. No longer was it necessary to drag a long cord along the ice while scraping.
- In 2006, Wood bought the Ice King business from Mayo and Veale. He currently sells four different models—the Prince, the Super Scraper, the Super 06, and the Super 07.
- Ice Kings have been used at virtually every major event from the Canadian men's and women's championships to the Olympics.
- Ice Kings are used around the world, and models some 30 years old are still used on a regular basis.

AMERICA'S MAN, BUD SOMERVILLE

Bud Somerville was the first American curler to skip a team to the world championship title, and in so doing he became the unofficial father of U.S. curling. A few facts about the legendary curler:

- He was a gifted athlete but a heart ailment kept him from playing most sports. As a result, he turned to curling.
- He first reached the U.S. finals in 1962, skipping a rink that included his father, Ray, at second, and his brother-in-law Bill Strum at lead. The team finished third.
- In the middle of the 1965 national final against a team from Illinois, Somerville's pants split up the front, and he was forced to patch them together with tape and a safety pin. Undaunted, he finished out the game, winning his first national title.
- The team became the first American rink—and first non-Canadian—to win the world championship when it captured the Scotch Cup in 1965. After the victory, the team received a telegram of congratulations from President Lyndon B. Johnson.
- He won a second world championship in 1974.
- Somerville's youngest son, John, died of cystic fibrosis at age 17, and Somerville has raised thousands and thousands of dollars for the research into the disease.

- In 1992, Somerville, at the age of 55, represented the United States at curling's demonstration at the Olympic Games, becoming that country's oldest Olympian. He skipped the rink to a bronze medal. He also skipped the team at the 1988 Games.
- When the U.S. Curling Hall of Fame was started in 1984, Somerville was the first inductee.
- His son Tim won three U.S. Championships and represented the United States in the 2002 Olympics.

Curling Quote

"Today I saw a bunch of Scotsmen who were throwing big iron balls like bombs on the ice, after which they cried, 'soop, soop,' and then laughed like mad.

I think they are mad."

—A French-Canadian farmer, circa 1790, relaying his first impressions of curling, as quoted in *The Curling Companion* by W.H. Murray

THE WRENCH SAID

He is one of the most beloved curlers of all time, and part of the reason for Ed Werenich's popularity was his penchant for speaking his mind, often saying something politically incorrect but that many were secretly thinking. Here is a selection of some of Werenich's most memorable quotes:

"They look like they're going jogging. Or maybe going to a pyjama party."

—Werenich commenting on the new-style athletic gear being worn by several European teams at the 1990 World Curling Championships

"I don't want him as my coach. I've worked 32 years for this moment. I don't want someone like him jumping in."

—Werenich, after winning the 1990 Brier, when he would not accept Canadian Curling Association official and longtime rival Warren Hansen as his team coach for the World Championships

"I went to Sweden, drank beer in my room, and came home with a bouquet of flowers and a $5 silver tray."

—Werenich summing up his experience at the 1990 World Championships in Vasteras, Sweden

"They not only want me to look pretty, they want me to be able to dance, too. I just hope they don't ask me to use Grecian Formula and get my teeth fixed."

—Werenich, when told he would have to lose 22 pounds and do aerobic exercise if he hoped to qualify for the 1987 Olympic trials

"How do you think this would look on my ass, Leon?"

—Werenich, while mooning Ontario Curling Association official Leon Sykes after Sykes had presented him with his Purple Heart for winning the 1981 Ontario championship. Werenich had battled officials all week over a problem with the playoff format.

"We went into this thing thinking we needed to be 8–3 to get into the playoffs. We've got the easy three over with. Now we have to go over the hard eight ones."

—Werenich at the 1984 Brier in Victoria after the defending champions started out 0–3

"They're four real jerks. I know where they can put their brooms."

—Werenich referring to the Swedish team in the 1983 World Championship, skipped by Mikael Hasselborg. The Swedes used messy corn brooms to sweep, a tactic Werenich believed was akin to cheating. For years after that incident, the Hasselborg team carried pictures of Werenich and teammate John Kawaja with them, saying they used them to get up for important games.

"When I'm on the curling ice, that's my office. I'll challenge anybody in the world on certain things, like calling strategy. I know curling, okay? But I really don't know anything else, just curling and firefighting."

—Werenich to author Jean Sonmor in the book *Burned By The Rock*

BETWEEN A ROCK AND
A HARD PLACE

In some places where curling isn't always a mainstream sport, curlers have had to make do with whatever they can to play their game. Here are a few unusual locations in which curling has been held:

- In 1992, the Imperial Grand Ballroom of the Aladdin Hotel and Casino in Las Vegas, Nevada, was transformed into a curling rink to host the Desert Spiel, a curling pro-am in which players competed on teams skipped by Canadian, U.S., and world champions. Curlers from across North America descended on Vegas to play in the event on ice made by world-renowned ice technician Shorty Jenkins.

- Vegas isn't the only place where curling has been held in a casino. In 2007, a made-for-television skins game was held in the Entertainment Centre at Casino Rama, near Orillia, Ontario. The location is usually reserved for singers and comedians, but the high-stakes shootout brought together Glenn Howard, Kevin Martin, Wayne Middaugh, and Brad Gushue.

- On more than one occasion, the skating rink in front of Rockefeller Center in New York City has been changed into a curling rink for an exhibition of the roaring game. In 2007, television personalities were given a lesson in curling by American Olympians Cassie Johnson and Pete Fenson in the heart of Manhattan.

- Curlers have been known to have the odd drink and so it might not be that big a surprise that a bonspiel was held in a location where some of this liquid is manufactured. No, not Scotland and Scotch, but California and wine. In 2007, a bonspiel was held in Vacaville, California, in the heart of Napa Valley. A local hockey rink was transformed into curling sheets, and the competitors threw rocks and sipped Merlot.

- According to the *International Guide to Curling* by Robin Welsh, in 1973, a bonspiel was held in Côte d'Ivoire in Africa. The event was held on an indoor rink in the Ivoire Hotel and included local teams as well as rinks from France. A second event was held and teams from Switzerland and the U.S.A. played.

- According to *The Curling News*, at a posh mall in Rabat, Morocco, the only skating rink in the country is regularly transformed into a curling rink and lessons provided to locals. Although most had never seen a skating rink before—let alone a game of curling— they weren't afraid to test it out, and thousands have given the game a go. Instead of scratching circles into the ice for rings, a system of lights is used to create the houses at either end of the sheet.

- In the 1880s, Scottish residents of New York held an annual bonspiel on a frozen pond in Central Park. The match pitted former residents of northern Scotland versus those from the south. The contest involved numerous teams, and scores were a total of all the games. In 1883, for example, the final score was North 182, South 150.

Curling in Vegas

CURLING COUPLES

Curling, as many who play will attest, is a social sport. For that reason, it's no big surprise that many curlers end up as couples, husbands and wives who share a love of rock tossing. Here are a few of the more successful curling couples.

Rick and Lorraine Lang: Lorraine Lang was a Canadian champion in 1988 and '89, and took the world title in 1989. Husband Rick is a three-time Brier winner—1972, '82, and '85—winning the world title in '82 and '85. Together, they captured the Canadian Mixed in 1981.

Dave and Heather Nedohin: Dave throws last rock for the powerful Randy Ferbey team that won four Canadian and three world championships, while Heather has a world junior and world women's title on her resumé.

Ian Tetley and Erica Brown: A cross-border couple. Ian Tetley is a three-time Canadian and world champion, while Erica has four U.S. women's titles to her credit, as well as two Olympic appearances.

Pat Perroud and Jane Hooper Perroud: Pat won Canadian and world championships playing lead for both Al Hackner (1985) and Ed Werenich (1990), while wife Jane was a member of Marilyn Bodogh's squad, which captured the Canadian and world championship in 1996.

Wayne and Sherry Middaugh: Wayne is a two-time Canadian and world champion while better half Sherry has won the Ontario title three times, reaching the semi-finals of the Canadian championship on all three occasions. Both curlers have competed in the Canadian Olympic curling trials.

Curling Quote

"They told us to watch out for odd people when he got here. The first guy I saw was wearing a gopher on his head. Where do you start?"

—A member of the security detail of Prime Minister Stephen Harper, who visited the 2007 Tim Hortons Brier in Hamilton, as told to the *Edmonton Sun*

ROCKS FOR ROCKERS

Members of the Canadian rock band The Tragically Hip are curling fans. That became obvious during a concert tour in 2006. The band was playing in London, Ontario, and singer/guitarist Ed Robertson told the assembled fans his tale of looking for curling stones so he could play on an outdoor rink he made each winter at his Ontario cottage. He had searched high and low, and finally found one company that made them—Canada Curling Stone, located in London, but when he called he only received an answering machine message, which he turned into a little song:

> *Canada Curling Stone*
> *Canada Curling Stone*
> *Please don't try to phone*
> *We're Canada Curling Stone*
> *No one is at home*
> *At Canada Curling Stone*
> *All of our rocks are home*
> *At Canada Curling Stone*
> *We implore you to leave us alone*
> *We're Canada Curling Stone*

The next morning, Robertson called the company again, and this time, Kim Tuck answered the phone, and when

Robertson introduced himself, she told him she'd already received scores of calls and e-mails from those who were at the concert the night before, relaying his request. In the end, that request was fulfilled, and Robertson bought a full sheet of 16 stones and reportedly has regular outdoor curling events at his cottage.

BRIER BROADCASTER

B ob Cole has made a career of calling hockey games. He's been the main play-by-play man for the CBC since 1980 and has been calling games for the network since 1973. He regularly calls the action for the Toronto Maple Leafs, and perhaps his most famous call came in 1976 during an exhibition game between the Philadelphia Flyers and the Russian club team CSKA Moscow. In the first period, the Russians became unhappy with the officiating and left the ice. From the press box, Cole said, "They're going home. They're going home."

While he became famous for that and more hockey broadcasting, Cole is also a curler of some note, having represented Newfoundland & Labrador in the Brier twice. In 1971 he finished up with a 4–6 mark, and in 1975 he went 1–10. Cole also skipped his province in the 1973 Canadian Mixed.

A FAMILY AFFAIR

Curling has always been considered a good family game, but at a 1998 bonspiel in Keene, Ontario, the Davises took that to a new level. The squad comprised Alan, Chris, Gord, and Jamie Davis—great-grandfather, grandfather, father, and son—four generations of the family all on one team.

HIGH SCORE

It is a badge of honour for every curler to play in the Brier and another to set records. While New Brunswick's Ken Everett might like to remember the former, he might not be too excited about the latter. Everett represented his province in the 1957 Brier in Kingston, which was won by Garnett Campbell's team from Saskatchewan. Along the way, Everett managed to put his team into the record books. Unfortunately it was for all the wrong reasons. The New Brunswick team came out on the wrong side of the most lopsided contest in Brier history—a 30–3 loss.

As well, in today's era of conceding games once the score seems insurmountable, it's unlikely that score will ever be topped.

TRAVELLIN' MAN

Earle Morris is a talented curler, but as a member of the Canadian military, he moved around the country a great deal. But that never hurt his success on the ice. Morris curled in the Brier three times, but represented three different provinces, the only player with such a distinction. In 1980, he represented Manitoba, in 1982 Quebec, and in '85 he wore Ontario's colours.

AGE-OLD INVENTION

Jack Grossart of Toronto proved that curling isn't necessarily the domain of the young man. He started curling at the age of 65 and fell in love with the sport. A self-confessed problem-solver, at age 89, he decided to try to invent a better curling broom and came up with the Grossart Super Brush. The innovative design was one of the first to feature a hinged head, which allowed it to be moved to any angle, and removable "friction pads" that could be switched depending on the ice conditions.

When asked why he started designing brooms at his age, he replied: "It's just stupidness. I wish I'd never got started in this thing." Grossart eventually sold off his broom business but kept curling until the age of 99.

GREAT COMEBACKS

Usually, teams that are ahead by healthy margins or with few ends to play don't surrender the lead. Most world-ranked rinks can finish off a game in which they lead by a few points. But on occasion, they slip up, allowing for a memorable comeback. Here are a few notable ones:

• In 1970, the ice at the Brier in Winnipeg was horrendous, and it contributed to a tremendous comeback by Hec Gervais. The ice was extremely heavy, and after four ends, Ontario's Paul Savage was leading 8–1. Starting in the fifth end, Gervais began calling for his team to draw to the outside rings, but they kept coming up light—or so thought Savage. Gervais intentionally placed the rocks in front of the rings, fooling the youthful Savage as the Alberta team rallied to a 12–9 win.

"I was thinking, 'These guys can't make a draw,'" recalled Savage. "Big mistake. I found out a few years after these were corner guards and did they ever work."

• Heading into the final three ends of the 2004 Brier, Nova Scotia's Mark Dacey trailed Randy Ferbey by four points and appeared to be headed for a silver medal. Certainly he was an underdog. Ferbey was gunning for his fourth consecutive Brier crown and seemed in control of this final. Undaunted, Dacey rallied for three in the eighth before surrendering a single in the ninth to trail by two heading home. But a combination of tremendous shots by the Nova Scotia rink and some stunning misses from the Ferbey team allowed Dacey to draw the four-foot for three points and a 10–9 victory.

- In the 2001 Canadian Olympic trials Russ Howard, trailing by three points with one end left, contemplated conceding a game against John Morris. The wily veteran, however, decided to play out the final frame, and what followed was a case of experience winning out over youth. Howard used a corner guard to hide several stones, and rather than removing the guard, Morris tried to pick out the Howard stones, but missed each time. Eventually, Howard took four points, winning the game and

sending Morris storming off the sheet, ripping his shirt into shreds in the process.

- Playing the tenth end of the final of the 1985 Brier in Moncton, New Brunswick, Pat Ryan was leading 5–3 and appeared in complete control of the final frame. In fact, after his last shot, he came down the ice with his broom in the air, already starting to celebrate what he thought was a Brier victory. However, that proved premature. Northern Ontario's Al Hackner played what is regarded as one of the greatest shots in Brier history when he made a thin double takeout to score two points. He then led his team to a steal of one in the extra end for the win and the Canadian championship.
- Ontario's Jenn Hanna was set to celebrate a victory in the 2005 Scott Tournament of

Hearts in St. John's, Newfoundland. With just one rock left to be thrown, Hanna led by three points and had shot stone buried on the button. Manitoba's Jennifer Jones sat second, third, and fourth shot but had only one hope of getting to Hanna's stone—that was to redirect her shooter off a stone sitting almost off the sheet. She called the shot, played it, and watched as it hit and then went on a perfect angle to remove the Ontario stone and give her team four points and the national title.

Curling Quote

"I worked with French CBC during the Torino Olympics. I did a TV show with a French-Canadian speed skater, and during that show, he tried some curling. At the end he looked at me and said, 'Geez guys...how do you do that? You guys are real athletes.'

Coming from a 29-year-old, two-time gold medalist in prime athletic condition, that's a very good compliment."

—Guy Hemmings in the *Penticton Western News*

PIZZA AND MEDALS

Pete Fenson was the skip of the first American team to win an Olympic medal in regulation play (American teams had earned medals in Olympic demonstrations). His rink, from Bemidji, Minnesota, took the bronze medal at the 2006 Games in Torino, Italy. As such, he became one of the best-known curlers in the United States. Here is a bit about this popular American curler:

- Fenson's father, Bob, won the United States Men's Championship in 1979. He taught Pete how to curl and has continued to serve as coach for the team.
- Fenson won his first national title in 1993, playing third for Scott Baird. He won again in 1994. He was a semi-finalist at the '93 world championship and finished fifth in '94.
- In 1998, Baird took a year off, and Fenson moved up to skip, learning under the watchful eye of veteran third Mark Haluptzok. In 2003, Fenson skipped his team to the U.S. title and then finished eighth at the world final.
- Fenson won the 2004 and '05 U.S. championships and then skipped the Red, White, and Blue to a bronze medal in the 2006 Games, earning that honour with an 8–6 victory over David Murdoch of the United Kingdom.
- The team was named the U.S. Olympic Committee's team of the year for 2006.

- Fenson owns two pizzerias, operating under the name Dave's Pizza.
- On the U.S. Olympic Committee website, Fenson was asked which cartoon character he best resembled. His answer was the Road Runner.
- In the summer of 2006, Fenson's Olympic team broke up as John Shuster, who played lead, left the squad to form his own rink.

OLE MEXICO

Curling isn't one of the more popular sports in Mexico, to be sure, but there are a few participants in the tropical country. In fact Josele Garza, a car racer who has participated in the Indy 500, is one of the country's original rock throwers.

After seeing the sport in the 1998 Olympics, he organized a group intent on setting up the sport in Mexico. The group travelled to Winnipeg for some instruction and a crash course on strategy. With only five arenas in Mexico City, it's difficult to get ice, but thanks to Garza and his group, there is an official curling club, and Mexico is a member country of the World Curling Federation.

LONG-GONE EQUIPMENT

It's been a long time since a straw broom appeared in any major competition around the world. In fact, straw brooms were last made in 2003, having succumbed to the success of the push broom. While only recently extinct, the straw broom is far from the only piece of equipment that has disappeared from the game over the years. Here are a few more items that were once common on curling rinks around the world.

Centre skittle

Years ago, before rings were permanently painted into the ice, a small wooden skittle was positioned at the exact centre of the ice. This allowed players at the throwing end of the sheet to have a visual idea of the location of the button.

Tassels

Hard as it may be to believe, many years ago, rocks weren't identified by coloured tops. That's primarily because each player was required to provide his or her own pair of stones, and there was no idea of what team he or she would be on for that game. Instead a small piece of coloured wool was tied to the handle—eight handles, actually—to determine which rocks belonged to which team.

Crampits

The name is perhaps more closely associated with mountain climbing, but a crampit (also called a crampon) was an attachment that was tied on to the bottom of a shoe or boot and had prongs on the underside that provided a hold on the ice. For a short time, players kept the crampit on their foot the entire game, while throwing and sweeping, which caused some horrendous conditions as they ran up and down the sheet. In later years, crampits were affixed to the ice and remained in position for the entire game, usually by putting the metal fixture into hot water and then melting it into the ice.

The Duster

The name came from the fact this was usually a cloth, much like something used for dusting. It was placed on the ice to show where the rock was to come to rest. If it was placed on top of a rock, the shot was a takeout.

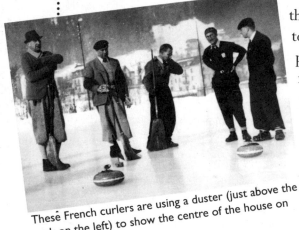

These French curlers are using a duster (just above the rock on the left) to show the centre of the house on this outdoor rink.

CLOSET CURLING FANS

Although they are better known for other endeavours, the three people listed below have a soft spot for the roaring game. It's just that nobody knew!

Wayne Gretzky—hockey's all-time scoring leader is a devoted curling fan who said he regularly follows the Brier and other events. And he admitted to another secret in a column he wrote in the *National Post*. "You'd be surprised how many National Hockey League players can be found sitting in their hotel rooms in the middle of winter watching [curling] somewhere."

Canadian Prime Minister Stephen Harper— Harper became the first prime minister to sit through an entire draw at the Brier, attending an afternoon at the 2007 event in Hamilton. Before the match, he met and had his photo taken with Kevin Martin's Alberta team. Harper, who said he's not a curler, still loves to watch the Canadian championship on a regular basis. "I've been following it for years and back about a decade ago when I was travelling a lot I happened to be in Winnipeg when they were having the Brier," he said, "and I made a point of going. Then I decided every year to schedule a business trip to be wherever the Brier was."

Toby Keith—the award-winning country singer said he fell in love with curling while following it at the 2006 Olympics. During a concert stop in Nashville, Tennessee, Keith decided he would take that passion one step further. He learned there was a curling facility in town and booked some ice for him and his band to play. "They're calling themselves the redneck curlers," commented Nashville Curling Club president Sean Gerster, who also admitted that Keith was a fast learner and showed promise. "He said he was going to try and qualify for the 2010 Olympics."

Bruce Springsteen—the Boss reportedly rents out curling clubs when on the road. He is known as a keen watcher of curling when it's on television, and is an improving rock tosser.

Curling Fact

The first European team to win the world championship was Kjell Oscarius of Sweden, who won in 1973.

SPRINGFIELD GRANITE

Curling went animated in 2002 when the sport was featured in an episode of *The Simpsons*. On February 17, episode 280-1311, "The Bart Wants What it Wants," aired on FOX and saw America's favourite animated family travel to Canada, where at one point Bart and his friend Millhouse start a fight in a movie/television studio. They brawl and eventually go through a door where a sign reads: *Curling for Loonies*, a reference to the American television staple, *Bowling for Dollars*. This Canadian show is being taped in the adjoining studio in which Bart and Millhouse now find themselves. As the two brawl, the announcers are heard:

Announcer 1: Well, we've seen some wild sweeping here today.
Announcer 2: Yes, the broom handling has been truly dazzling. [At this point, Bart and Milhouse are seen fighting their way onto the ice.] What's this? Two young Yankee Doodles have turned this match into a Dandy.
Announcer 1: [laughs] Both our viewers must be thrilled. A very special episode of *Curling for Loonies*.

THE CURSE OF LABONTE

One of the more unusual finishes to a major curling competition took place in 1972 at the world championships in Garmish-Partenkirchen, Germany. The final was between Canada's Orest Meleschuk and Bob Labonte of the United States. Up to that point, Canada was undefeated and hoping to run the table in the final. Heading to the tenth end, the Americans led by two points, but Meleschuk had the hammer.

In order to score two points, Meleschuk needed to hit and stay inside the eight-foot. He played the shot, but the shooter apparently rolled too far, giving the game to the Americans. Frank Assand, the U.S. third, who had been sweeping the Canadian shooter as it rolled, judged where that rock had stopped and where his team's shooter sat and immediately threw his hands in the air. His skip, Labonte, also believing they had won, jumped into the air in celebration, but slipped and kicked the Canadian stone, moving it back toward the centre of the rings. Now it appeared Canada had scored the tying deuce. After consulting with the head official, Doug Maxwell, a measurement took place, and Canada scored two then went on to win the game in the extra end.

A few more notes about the infamous burned rock:

- At the time, there were no rules in place to deal with the situation that occurred. Maxwell was left with little option but to leave the rocks where they were and measure the burned stone and the American rock.
- To show how the times have changed, Labonte managed to complete his jump and tumble all with a cigarette in his mouth.
- In his book *Canada Curls*, Maxwell revealed that the CBC, which was covering the event, had just introduced instant replay and was supposed to have it available at the world championship, but a labour dispute cancelled its availability.
- A reporter came up with the Labonte Curse, supposedly dropped on Canadian curlers. The idea was the country would never win another world championship, the revenge for winning the 1972 event under such strange circumstances. For the next seven years, Canada didn't win the global title, its longest dry spell.
- For many years, Labonte showed up at world championships, introduced himself to the Canadian team, and playfully put the hex on them again.
- After the incident, Labonte was given the nickname "Boots."

BRITISH GOLD

When Rhona Martin took top spot in the 2002 Olympics in Salt Lake City, Utah, the win set off a wild celebration back in Scotland (her country of residence) and across Great Britain. Some remarkable facts about Martin and that victory:

- Prior to being selected to represent Britain at the Olympics, Martin had made it to 10 national championships and finished second a remarkable nine times. She did represent Scotland at the European championships but lost in the semi-finals five of six times and subsequently lost all five bronze medal games.
- More than 7 million viewers in Britain tuned into the broadcast of the gold medal game even though it started at midnight local time. That set a record for the BBC.
- It was the first gold medal for Britain in 19 Olympiads.
- Martin and her team of Janice Ranin, Fiona Macdonald, and Debbie Knox became household celebrities across Britain, even receiving MBEs. However, their fame was fleeting. Five years later, Martin was living in part off social security after her husband left her. She later gained a job as a curling instructor.

IRON CURLING

While granite stones are the traditional implements of use in curling games around the world, it hasn't always been that way.

From 1807 until the early 1920s in Quebec and the Ottawa Valley, curling "irons" were the choice—markers made of metal that weighed up to 80 pounds. According to the book *Sports and Games in Canadian Life, 1700 to the Present*, Maxwell L. Howell and Nancy Howell suggest that the first of these irons were derived from the metal-rimmed hubcaps of gun carriages. Handles were inserted into these to turn them into curling "stones."

It was only in this area that irons were used, and one of the reasons they disappeared was a financial gesture of the Macdonald Tobacco Company. It wanted to start a national curling championship and needed Quebec curlers to participate. To entice them, the tobacco company spent thousands of dollars to buy granite stones for many curling clubs in Quebec, easing the transition to the rock era.

BROTHERS—AND SISTERS—IN BROOMS

Curling siblings have been common sights atop the podiums of major events, showing that perhaps the ability to draw the button is genetic. Here are some of the more successful curling siblings:

Russ and Glenn Howard: The duo won two world championships together, and separately they've also been successful. Russ was a part of Brad Gushue's gold medal-winning squad at the 2006 Olympics, while Glenn won a third world crown skipping his own team in 2007.

Julie and Jodi Sutton: The two won the Canadian championship in 1991, five years after combining to capture the national junior crown. Julie also has a bronze medal from the 2002 Olympics.

Jim and Tom Wilson: The Wilson brothers were a feared front end in the late 1970s and early '80s, sweeping for Rick Folk's Saskatchewan rink. They helped the team win a Canadian and world championship in 1980.

Ernie and Sam Richardson: Two members of the famed Richardson rink from Saskatchewan, which won four Briers in five years. Ernie was the skip while Sam (whose real name was Garnet) played second. Two other cousins, Arnold and Wes, were also members of the rink.

Ken and Grant Watson: These brothers paired up to win three Brier crowns between 1936 and 1949, a record for siblings.

Connie, Corinne, and Janet Laliberte: With Connie at skip, these three sisters swept their way to the Canadian championship in 1984. Connie and Janet combined for two more titles as well.

The Campbells

The Campbells: Don, Garnett, Lloyd, and Sam won the 1954 Brier playing out of Saskatchewan. It's the only time four brothers have combined on a team to win a national championship.

Cassie Potter and Jamie Haskell: The sisters from Bemidji, Minnesota, have been U.S. champions and represented their nation at the Olympics.

TANKARD TOTAL

When Labatt took over sponsorship of the Brier in 1980, it needed a trophy of some sort to present and decided that a budget of $5,000 would deliver it a suitable award. Labatt's Grant Waterman was put in charge of the job and he commissioned what would become a piece of Canadian sporting history, the Labatt Tankard, a large gold stein with the company's logo on the front. He managed to keep the trophy hidden from press and even his co-workers until an unveiling at a press conference in Calgary, site of the 1980 Brier, where the Tankard would be presented for the first time. When it was revealed to the press, the reaction was positive, and as photographers snapped away, Labatt vice-president Sid Oland sidled over to Waterman and congratulated him on the trophy.

"How much did it cost?" he asked.

"$35,000," said Waterman.

Shocked, Oland asked what happened to the $5,000 budget.

"The case cost $10,000," Waterman exclaimed.

While there were a lot of upset people in the Labatt financial department, the move paid off a few years later when the Tankard was valued at $350,000.

CHAMPIONSHIPS FOR EVERYONE

The Tim Hortons Brier and Scotties Tournament of Hearts are well known as the men's and women's Canadian championships, respectively. But there are plenty more national titles up for grabs each year.

Canadian Postal Employees Curling Championship

Started in 1967 in Winnipeg, this event was originally known as the Canadian Postal Curling Championship. It's been held annually and has teams from every province and a combined territories entry.

Royal Canadian Legion

First held in 1957, the Legion's spiel is known as the Dominion Championship and is open to members of the Royal Candian Legion.

Canadian Firefighters Curling Association

This group not only has a championship but a full-blown association. It was started by Aubrey Neff, who started a curling league among members of the Vancouver Fire Department. He contacted firefighters in other provinces, and in 1960, a championship was held between five provinces. Today, all ten provinces, Northern Ontario, and the territories compete. Past winners include Ed Werenich and Neil Harrison.

Canadian Blind Curlers Championship

Ten teams play down for this championship. Some represent cities and others provinces, while the defending champion enters as Team Canada.

Canadian Clergy Championship

This competition—known as the Friar's Brier—had its start in 1978 and is for members of the Canadian clergy and their associates. It is held annually in the same city as the real Brier.

Canadian Police Curling Championship

Back in 1955, the Canadian Association of Chiefs of Police formed the Canadian Police Curling Association. In 1956, a "national bonspiel" was held at the Winnipeg Granite Club, and in 1972, it was transformed into a true national championship.

The Trans-Canada Telephone Employees' Championship

Regina played host to the first national championship in 1964. Seven provinces currently compete for the title.

The Atlantic Oilworkers Championship

Anyone who gets a paycheque from the Atlantic petroleum industry is eligible for this championship, which celebrated its 44th anniversary in 2008.

FANTASTIC FERBEY

Randy Ferbey has won more Briers than any other curler, a total of six. He won twice while playing for Pat Ryan (1988 and '89) and has earned four more titles as skip of his own team in the 2000s. Although he calls the game, third player David Nedohin throws last rock. A few notes on Randy Ferbey:

- He appeared on a television commercial for sponsor Strauss Herbs looking somewhat like a raccoon. The day before the taping, he had been at his son's baseball tournament, spending the day outside wearing wrap-around sunglasses. He forgot to apply sunscreen, and his face went red, except for where he was protected by his glasses. He gained notoriety for his appearance…and ribbing from just about every opponent, not to mention his teammates.
- Ferbey's team holds the record for scoring the most points in a single end at the world championship—five, a mark he achieved twice during the 2005 world final.
- His team of Nedohin, Scott Pfeifer, and Marcel Rocque became the first to win four Briers with the same lineup. The famed Richardsons of Saskatchewan also won four, but on one occasion had a different lead.
- His team was the first to have a book written about it. *The Ferbey Four* was written by Edmonton sportswriter Terry Jones.

- He was one of the few high-profile curlers not to join a 2001 movement of teams that elected to play in the Grand Slam of Curling instead of the Brier. That set him apart from many of his peers, but he said at the time: "Maybe to some of the players [the Grand Slam is] right up there but let's be honest. To the paying public the Brier is the event of the year. I don't care what anybody else says."
- He appeared, along with lead Marcel Rocque, on the television program *Celebrity Chefs*, where he showed off his prowess in the kitchen by preparing shrimp canapés with homemade mayo and dill, smoked goose breast canapés, pork loin chops (brined) with a port/maple/nut reduction, lightly steamed vegetables in garlic/olive oil sauce. Rocque did most of the cooking.
- Along with teammate Dave Nedohin, he made a cameo appearance on the television program *Corner Gas*, playing himself.

ROARING ALONG

Curling is known at "the roaring game." This moniker was given to the sport for the sound the stones made as they travelled down the ice. While rocks don't particularly roar these days on artificial playing surfaces in clubs, there was a definite hum when the sport was played outdoors on the frozen lochs of Scotland, and that's where the name originated.

PLANES, TRAINS, AND AUTOMOBILES

Curlers are certainly a determined bunch, but Rob Whalen and his rink from Sioux Lookout, Ontario, took that to extremes en route to the 1996 northwestern Ontario playdowns.

They had originally booked seats on a flight from their hometown to Thunder Bay, hoping to arrive the morning of the start of the competition. However, that morning, a massive snowstorm hit the area, closing the airport. Undaunted, the team piled into a four-by-four and started off on the 250-kilometre trek. At Ignace, Ontario, about halfway to their destination, police had closed the road, forcing the team to find yet another way.

Whalen, who worked on the railway, headed to the rail yards and managed to convince the crew of a freight train headed to Thunder Bay to let them board. But that didn't work either, as the blizzard forced the train to stop and back up to Ignace to wait out the weather.

Back into the four-by-four the team members went, and this time, Whalen drove an hour southwest to Fort Frances and then finally on to Thunder Bay, arriving at 4:30 a.m., having missed his first two games in the triple-knockout competition. To add to the disaster, after winning their first two games, the team lost in its third contest, one victory short of qualifying for the provincial final.

HOLEY SLIDER

It may have been inexperience, it could have been just a case of being naive, but Lino Di Iorio changed the way people slide just two years after taking up the sport.

Di Iorio is the creator of the BalancePlus Slider, an invention that stopped an age-old problem with Teflon sliders.

After taking up the sport at 45, Di Iorio no-

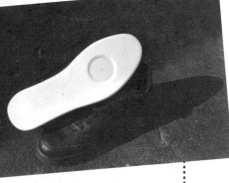

ticed that the slider on his curling shoe had curled up so the edges weren't on the ice surface. Looking at other players' shoes, he noticed it was a common problem. "To me, it showed that although the foot is about four inches wide, people were only sliding on about two inches of that."

Combining his background in physics with an affinity for solving problems, he created the new slider, which has a shallow hole in the centre of it.

"Most people just slide on the ball of their foot," Di Iorio said. "By adding the hole, that part of the slider doesn't come into contact with the ice. In essence, the person's weight is spread out over a greater area."

The BalancePlus Slider was first used by players such as Kevin Martin and Ed Werenich, who raved about it. That led to a surge in demand for the slider with the hole in it, and Di Iorio's invention has become the best-selling slider in the game.

QUITE AN ORDER

Three Canadian curlers have been honoured with the Order of Canada, the highest civilian honour in the country. They are:

Ken Watson (invested 1975)
Ron Northcott (invested 1976)
Ernie Richardson (invested 1978)

THE WRENCH
VS. THE WENCH

It was billed as the Battle of the Sexes, and while there have been many male-versus-female curling games, none were as high profile as one that took place in 1986 between Marilyn Darte, at that time the reigning women's world champion, and Ed Werenich, the 1983 world champ and one of the top curlers of the day. Darte (now Bodogh) appeared on a sports talk show and, feeling confident, issued the challenge to Werenich, which he accepted.

The match was held during the world championships, which were being contested in Toronto. In the lead-up to the game, the two—who never met a reporter they didn't like—playfully tossed barbs back and forth. They appeared on national television and on the front page of national newspapers. A few notes about the infamous match:

- The game drew the largest crowd of the week at the world championships with a sold-out audience in excess of 7,000.
- Both teams came onto the ice by bursting through huge paper hearts—purple for the men, red for the women. Boxer Shawn O'Sullivan, then at the height of his career—led the way for the Werenich rink, while Bodogh's team came out turning cartwheels.

- Werenich's teammates came out wearing firefighters' helmets with flashing lights and blaring sirens, while Werenich came through wearing a crown and cape. The cape was being carried by an extremely busty woman in a short skirt.
- Werenich's usual third, Paul Savage, was replaced by Northern Ontario's Rick Lang for the game. During the fifth-end break, Savage led a parade of women, dressed in aprons and cooks' hats and banging pots and pans, around the ice surface.
- At one point, a CCA official appeared and jokingly called Darte third Kathy McEdwards for a hog line violation. Instead of removing the rock, however, he picked up McEdwards and carried her off the sheet.
- The contest was broadcast live on TSN and received a rating higher than any games from that week's world championship.
- The men won the game 11–3, with the women only scoring in the last end.
- A rematch was held in 1996, during the world championships, but it never grabbed the attention of the initial contest.

STICKING TO CURLING

Curling has a great record of being accessible to all, with regular championships for blind, wheelchair, and deaf players. But one of the greatest inventions for keeping people in the game has been known simply as the Stick.

The Stick is a pole with an attachment at the end that fits over the handle of the rock. It allows a player to deliver a stone without having to bend down in the hack to do so, allowing plenty of players with back problems to continue at the game.

The History of the Stick

Several people claim to be the original inventor of the Stick, but most lean towards Preston Featherstone of Hamilton, Ontario, as the originator. Featherstone started curling in 1960 and for many years played alongside his friend Wilber House. The two often played as many as 25 bonspiels each winter, developing a long-lasting friendship.

In 1992, at the age of 82, House developed arthritis in his back, which left him unable to curl, a situation that led him—according to Featherstone—to become irritable and depressed.

In desperation, Featherstone decided he needed to find a way to get his friend back curling, and he got his idea from one of House's other passions. When he wasn't curling, House was a noted shuffleboard player in Tampa, Florida, routinely reaching the finals of tournaments where five hundred experienced players entered. Borrowing on that idea and from a welding-rod holder he had invented for business many years prior, Featherstone developed a stick with an attachment at the end that fit over the rock handle with a hinge. House took to the stick, named the Featherstone CurlMaster, model Mark 1, and was soon back curling.

Refinements have been made over the years, and other manufacturers have jumped into the game with their own models. The Stick even made an appearance at the Brier. In 2000, Northern Ontario alternate Paul Sauve played two shots in a game using his Stick. Shortly after that appearance, the device was banned in events leading to a national championship by the Canadian Curling Association. However, many jurisdictions around the world have separate Stick championships. More important, the invention by Featherstone has allowed many curlers with back and knee problems to continue playing.

NO RESPECT

Curlers have always had a hard time being treated seriously by mainstream media. Two examples:

- It's not very often that the U.S. mainstream press covers curling, but a 1994 report in *USA Today* on the Buffalo Bills did so—in a backhanded manner. The story centred on how the Bills have become synonymous with losing in sport. It provided quotes from other areas of sports and business where the Bills—who lost four consecutive Super Bowls—were used as an analogy for losing. One was provided by Russ Howard when he won the 2001 Brier after losses in the previous two. "I don't want to be compared to the Buffalo Bills," said Howard. The story then followed with this line: "So it has come to this... The Bills are getting goofed on by curlers."

- A newspaper ad in the *Toronto Sun* for a pay-per-call sports handicapping service carried the following headline: "You could earn big money in sports, with no noticeable athletic ability (just like pro curlers)." The service later offered an apology and stopped the ad.

SLIPS OF THE TONGUE

Putting microphones on players during televised curling games goes back to the 1960s when it was done
for the CBC Curling Classic. While it provides first-hand
insight into the strategy of players, it also has all the in-
herent dangers of live audio. Here are a few of the more
memorable microphone moments from curling:

Winnipeg curler Orest Meleschuk was known for his
foul language, and during coverage of a major cash bonspiel
in Sudbury, Ontario, local viewers got a first-hand taste. At
one point during the game, the big skip found himself in a
tight situation with no apparent way out. He turned to his
third, John Usackis—and in the process, the television audience—and said: "What the fuck are we going to do here
John, eh? What the fuck are we going to do? What the fuck
are we going to do?"

In the 1983 Brier, also in Sudbury, Ed Werenich
and Paul Savage were discussing Werenich's final shot.
Werenich said to Savage, in a comment that was picked
up by the CBC microphones: "I'll throw it narrow and let
the boys sweep the piss out of it."

A year later, in the final of the 1984 Brier, Werenich's
Ontario team was facing Mike Riley of Manitoba. Savage
was suffering some stomach problems, and during the
fifth end, he raced to the washroom, forgetting

completely that he was still wearing his microphone. Luckily the CBC was in a commercial break, but the staff in the production truck heard all the strange noises of Savage's visit to the washroom.

RECORD MAN

As one of the most successful curlers in history, Russ Howard's name is understandably all over the Brier record book. Here are a few of his and his team's entries:

Most appearances*	13
Most wins*	107
Most losses*	56
Most games played*	163
Most games as skip*	163
Most blank ends in a game (1993)	8
Lowest combined score (1993)	2–1
Shortest game (1986)	4 ends (Howard won 11–0)

*individual records

WHY HURRY?

Canadian, world, and Olympic champion Russ Howard is probably the best-known caller of sweeping instructions in the game. His famous call of "Hurry hard," usually heard at a high decibel level, is as famous as any in the game. Here's how it came about:

When Howard started skipping in the late 1970s, one of the most popular brooms was called the Rink Rat, a foam-synthetic model that caused a huge amount of noise, making it hard to hear when there were multiple games going on at the same time.

Out of necessity, Howard came up with a phrase that would distinguish him from other skips who yelled "Sweep," so his teammates could hear him above the din. He decided on "Hurry hard," which stuck.

Not everyone enjoyed hearing Howard yell— which he did almost incessantly during major events— and people told him in e-mails and face-to-face meetings. But most of them only had to listen for a few games. Longtime Howard second, Wayne Middaugh, got so used to listening to it during the five years he played for him, he had personalized licence plates made that read: "HURREE."

CURLING NICKNAMES

Terry Braunstein

Curlers have some of the most colourful nicknames in sport, a few of which can even be written in a family book. Here are the real names and nicknames of a number of Brier champions:

Curler	Nickname
Ed Werenich ('83, '90)	The Wrench
Orest Meleschuk ('72)	The Big O
Paul Savage ('83)	The Round Mound of Come Around
Al Hackner ('82, '85)	The Ice Man
Kevin Martin ('91, '97)	K-Mart
Ed Lukowich ('78, '86)	Cool Hand Luke
Barry Fry ('79)	The Snake
Rod Hunter ('70, '71)	The Arrow
Ron Manning ('67)	Moon
Terry Braunstein ('65)	Bronco
Ray Turnbull ('65)	Moosey

PERFECT RECORD

G etting through the Brier with a perfect record is a nearly impossible feat. In fact, in almost 80 years only 13 rinks have managed perfect records.

Randy Ferbey	13–0	2003
Pat Ryan	12–0	1988
Ron Northcott	10–0	1969
Matt Baldwin	10–0	1957
Garnet Campbell	10–0	1955
Billy Walsh	10–0	1952
Don Oyler	10–0	1951
Ken Watson	9–0	1949
Jimmy Welsh	9–0	1947
Howard Wood	9–0	1940
Ab Gowanlock	9–0	1938
Leo Johnson	7–0	1934
Gordon Hudson	9–0	1929

BABY BROTHER

While he might not have as much notoriety as his older brother Russ, Glenn Howard has enjoyed a great deal of success on the ice as well. A look at the career of Glenn Howard:

- Glenn is six years younger than Russ.
- Glenn has won three Canadian and world championships, one more than Russ.
- While playing for his brother during the 1980s and early '90s, Glenn had a tremendous rivalry with Ed Werenich, with no love lost between the two. However, he later spent one year curling for Werenich after Russ moved to New Brunswick.
- Howard made a guest appearance on the CBC comedy series *Little Mosque on the Prairie*. He played himself and was overlooked when the characters on the program were choosing sides for a big curling match. At first, the producers wanted to cast Kevin Martin in the spot, but the first assistant director, a former Canadian junior champion named Dave Manion, convinced them that Howard would be better.
- His full-time job is running the Beer Store in Midland, Ontario.
- In 2006–07, his team wore pink shirts and swept with pink-handled brooms as part of an awareness and fundraising effort for breast cancer.
- Along with teammates Richard Hart, Brent Laing, and Craig Savill, he started a fantasy curling camp to allow curlers of all abilities to mix with and learn from the world champions.

PLAY THE GAME

Russ Howard has played the most Brier games in the history of the Canadian championship with 163. And second on the list? His younger brother, Glenn.

Here is a ranking of the curlers who have played the most games up to 2007.

Curler	Briers	Games Played
Russ Howard	13	163
Glenn Howard	9	115
Pat Ryan	9	109
Al Hackner	9	106
Randy Ferbey	8	100
Kevin Martin	8	100
Rick Lang	9	99
Don Walchuk	8	97
Peter Gallant	8	89
Ed Werenich	7	89
Robert Campbell	9	88
Wayne Middaugh	7	88
Don Bartlett	8	85
Pierre Charette	9	85
Grant Odishaw	7	81
Mark O'Rourke	9	79
Neil Harrison	7	77
Jeff Stoughton	6	74
Bruce Lohnes	6	73
Mark Butler	7	70
Don Westphal	6	68
Mark Dacey	5	65
John Kawaja	6	65
Scott Pfeifer	5	65

HEAD(SET) GAMES

The 1989 Brier in Saskatoon saw one of the most unusual and infamous incidents in the history of the Canadian championship. Russ Howard, the Ontario skip and a notorious yeller when it came to shouting out sweeping instructions, began to lose his voice. Between the noise on the other sheets and the crowd, his sweepers were having trouble hearing his squeaky voice. To alleviate the problem, Howard elected to use voice-activated walkie-talkie headsets hoping he could communicate with front-end players Tim Belcourt and Kent Carstairs. Belcourt wore the second unit, and Carstairs picked up the sweeping instructions from him. The system worked and the Ontario team won its contest, but after the game, Howard was told by Canadian curling officials he wasn't allowed to use them. He asked what rule it violated, and when told there wasn't an infraction, he brought the headsets out for the next game.

Here are a few more facts about the incident.

- In the first end of the first game with the headsets, Glenn Howard was narrow with a shot, and Russ yelled quickly and with force, and for some reason, his full voice kicked in. Over the microphone, the call nearly blew off Tim Belcourt's ear.
- Prior to the second game, Pat Ryan of Alberta came over to see what all the commo-

tion was and asked Howard how the units worked. With Belcourt at the other end of the ice, Howard said softly into the headset, "Hey Tim, how big is your thing?" Belcourt immediately raised his hands over his head, holding them apart about three feet. Ryan laughed.

- One argument the CCA officials gave to Howard as to why he shouldn't be allowed to use the walkie-talkies was that someone in the crowd could be relaying information to him. When that was relayed to the press, one asked smartly, "And just what is someone in the stands going to tell Russ Howard?"

- After the next game, an RCMP officer faxed Howard and told him he'd lend him a wireless unit that wouldn't be seen by any CCA official.

- Before every draw, Howard was handed several homemade remedies for his laryngitis by fans, and he was given throat lozenges by the basket full.

- Howard ended up using the headsets for two games, after which his voice returned.

Curling Quote

"[It's] one of the very few sports that combine the excitement of a heavy piece of granite sliding slowly across the ice with the excitement of chunky broom-wielding people in bowling attire sweeping furiously in the stone's path, like janitors on speed."

—*Miami Herald* columnist Dave Barry on curling after viewing it at the 2002 Olympics

GOING LOW

Prince Edward Island is Canada's smallest province, and when it comes to the Brier, it's also the smallest on the scoreboard. The record for the combined low score in a Brier game is three—games that ended 2–1. That's happened on three occasions, and all three times, it has involved teams from Prince Edward Island, all of whom came out on the wrong end of the score.

In 2000, Andrew Robinson lost to Manitoba's Jeff Stoughton, in 1993 Ontario's Russ Howard defeated Robert Campbell, and in 1990, Ted MacFadyen came up short against Jim Sullivan of New Brunswick. In the latter two games, the teams combined for eight blank ends, also a Brier record.

THE MAGICAL 8

The eight-ender is the mark of perfection in curling—every rock in the rings and counting. It's often compared to the hole-in-one in golf, but it's exceedingly more difficult because, in golf, your opponent doesn't try to keep you from scoring an ace. For an eight-ender, not only does one team have to make eight perfect shots, but the opposition has to miss as well.

For that reason, it's rare to see an eight-ender in competitive play. But it has happened. At the 2006 Players Championship, the finale of the World Curling Tour, Kelly Scott of Kelowna, British Columbia, led her team to a perfect eight over Edmonton's Cathy King. Here's how the last four rocks played out:

1. Scott has six rocks in the rings, five counting. Four are in or touching the four-foot and another is on the eight-foot. The sixth rock is at the top of the rings, half in the twelve-foot. King has fifth shot fully in the twelve-foot at the ten o'clock position. With her first shot, King attempts to lightly tap back the shot rock at the top of the button but comes heavy, misses everything, and sails through the house.

2. Scott plays a guard that stops at the top of the rings, half in the twelve-foot.

3. King's only option is to try and redirect her shooter, playing a hit on her own stone. She hits her own rock too thick, spills across the

rings, touching two Scott stones but then exiting the house, leaving Scott an open draw for eight.

4. Scott's shot is slightly heavy but stops in the back of the house for eight points.

BIG ROCKS

The town of Arborg, Manitoba, lays claim to having the world's largest curling rock. Located 100 kilometres north of Winnipeg, the town of 1,021 erected the stone in 2006 in hopes of using it as a drawing card for passersby. The stone weighs in at a tonne and a half, measures 4.2 metres across and 2.1 metres tall and is made of steel, foam, and fibreglass.

This oversized rock is just a little bigger than the previous record holder located in Thunder Bay, Ontario. Known as the Lakehead Rock, that stone, which measures in at six and a half feet high and almost six feet in diameter and is made of concrete, was built to celebrate the 1960 Brier held in Thunder Bay. It held the record for more than 40 years, and many residents weren't impressed with being overtaken by the Arborg stone. When asked about the new record holder, Alf Childs, the Thunder Bay stone's caretaker, told the Thunder Bay *Chronicle Journal*: "That's an affront to granite right there."

STONE CUTTER

There are only two places in the world still making curling stones. One is Canada Curling Stone Company, located in London, Ontario. Over the years, it has refined the art of making stones and produces wonderful rocks that are used all over the world.

Here is a brief, step-by-step plan of how a stone is made:

1. Huge blocks of granite are located from a quarry in Wales. This quarry produces granite that has a very fine grain and has little or no quartz in it, the desired type for curling rocks. This granite has greater impact resistance than regular granite.

2. The block is cut down into smaller slabs from which large plugs, just larger than a curling stone, are cut. These plugs are shipped to Canada Curling Stone.

3. The first step for the plugs once they reach Canada is to have the centre hole cut through them. The hole is roughly half an inch in width.

4. The sides of the plug are then rounded off so it more closely resembles the shape of the stone.

5. Once the sides have been rounded, a small pocket on the bottom of the stone is cut out to allow for an insert to be put in place. The inserts often come from older rocks whose running surface has worn out. By cutting up these older stones of fine Scottish granite, inserts can be created. These inserts provide a better running surface for the stone and extend its life.

6. Once the insert has been affixed, a cup is created in both the top and bottom of the stone to allow the small running edge to be the only part of the stone that touches the ice.

7. The stone is then polished with diamond abrasive pads. The bottom is also run over sandpaper to give it more grit to allow it to grab the ice better.

8. The striking band is put on next by blasting the stone under high pressure with glass beads.

9. Finally a handle is attached to the stone, and it's ready for play.

OLYMPIC DOUBLE

In 1924, curling made its debut at the Winter Olympics held in Chamonix, France. A few notes about that competition:

- Four teams played in the competition: France, Great Britain, and two rinks from Sweden.
- The games were 18 ends in length and played outdoors.
- Britain, which was represented by a group of Scots, won its two games, defeating Sweden I 38–7 and knocking off France 46–4.
- The two Swedish teams did not play each other and so there was a playoff for the silver medal between France and Sweden II, which the Swedes won. Remarkably, both Swedish teams were awarded silver medals while the French took the bronze.
- In the playoff, Major D.G. Astley of Great Britain played for Sweden II. He was awarded a silver medal for leading that team to a win and also took home a gold medal as part of the British team, making him the only person in Olympic history ever to win two medals in the same event.
- For many years, the competition was viewed as merely a demonstration and not an official event. However, an investigation by *The Herald*, a Glasgow newspaper, showed the 1924 curling competition was, at the time, seen as official. In 2006, the International Olympic Committee upgraded the status of that curling playdown from demonstration to official.
- Curling was held at the Olympics several times since the 1924 Games, but never as an official event. It was reinstated in 1998 in Nagano, Japan.

ROCK HARD SUCCESS

Newfoundland and Labrador has won just a single Brier title since joining the competition in 1951. That win came in 1976 when a team led by skip Jack MacDuff beat remarkable odds to capture the Canadian championship. For many years, the rinks from Newfoundland and Labrador were viewed as hapless pushovers, having compiled a win-loss record of 45–206 prior to '76. Here are some of the highlights of that historic victory.

- The team's driver for the week was none other than Sam Richardson, of the famed Richardson family team that won four Briers. He not only drove the team but guided them through the ups and downs of the week, serving more as a coach than chauffeur.
- Curling fans in Newfoundland and Labrador became almost rabid as the team kept winning games. The MacDuff team received so many telegrams that the bellboys were carrying them to their room by the armload, and the telegrams managed to cover every square inch of wall space in one of the team's hotel rooms.
- Newfoundland Premier Frank Moores called the team midweek and said down the line, "A lot of people here don't know a thing about curling, but they're going crazy anyway."
- The last game of the round robin was against Ontario, and a

win would give Newfoundland the Brier. In the 10th end of a 12-end game, Ontario gave up a steal of 3 to give MacDuff a 9–3 lead. Ontario skip Joe Gurowka went to concede the game and the title to the Newfoundlanders, but Doug Maxwell of the CBC came out and said, "You have to keep playing, this game is on television and we've got another hour to go."

• Prior to skipping his own team, MacDuff played three years for Bob Cole, best known as the longtime hockey broadcaster for CBC.

• Following the win, MacDuff had his curling shoes bronzed and put on display at the St. John's Curling Club.

• The team didn't fare so well at that year's world championship, compiling a record of 2–9, the worst by a Canadian rink.

• So well known was Jack MacDuff's win, he received a congratulatory card from Western Canada addressed simply to "Jack MacDuff, Newfoundland."

• The team's third, Toby McDonald, served as coach for Brad Gushue's team, which won the gold medal at the 2006 Olympics.

HAMMER TIME

Last rock is supposed to be a significant advantage to top teams, but that's not always the case. In 1986, Alberta's Ed Lukowich recorded an 11–0 win over Newfoundland's Fred Durant, and Lukowich stole all 11 points.

GOING LONG

If a curling game goes long, expect Northern Ontario to come out on top. The record for the longest game in Brier history is 15 ends, which has happened twice. In 1927, the Brier's first year, all games were 14 ends. Twice, Northern Ontario had to go to an extra end to determine a winner. The first came against Toronto while the second was in a match against Quebec. Northern Ontario won both times by a score of 11–10.

THE REAL WORLD

Unlike most other top athletes, top curlers usually hold down full-time jobs and try to combine curling and work. Some players have rather unusual vocations. Here's a look at some notable curlers and their full-time occupations:

Colleen Jones	weather/sports presenter, CBC
Ed Werenich	firefighter
Wayne Middaugh	golf professional
Markku Uusipaavalniemi	Member of Parliament, Finland
Glenn Howard	beer store manager
Peter Corner	police officer
Vic Peters	golf course superintendent
Pete Fenson	pizza parlour owner
Hammy Macmillan	hotel manager

WORLD SERIES CURLER

New Zealand curler Hans Frauenlob is the only player to compete in the World Curling Championships and have two Major League Baseball World Series rings. Huh, you say?

Frauenlob, a competitive curler originally a Torontonian, worked for the Toronto Blue Jays in their IT department during the club's 1992 and 1993 World Series victories. As was every other Blue Jay employee, he was presented with a World Series ring after each of the club's wins.

He later moved to New Zealand where he continued his curling career, eventually making it all the way to the world championship.

MARKKU THE MAGNIFICENT

Markku Uusipaavalniemi is best known for winning a silver medal for Finland at the 2006 Olympics. But he has been around the game for a long time and worked harder than most to reach world-class status. Some things you might not know about Uusipaavalniemi:

- In 2007 he was elected to Finland's Parliament.
- U.S. curler Pete Fenson nicknamed him M-15 because he was unable to pronounce his last name. He has also been called Uusialphabet.
- As a student, he once had the highest mathematics score in a nationwide test and has reportedly solved a Rubik's Cube in 25 seconds.
- Following his silver medal at the Olympics, more than 1,000 people turned up for weekly clinics, encouraged by his team's performance. He was fielding 150 e-mails a day and appeared on television weekly.
- Uusipaavalniemi played in the 2002 Olympics, finishing fifth. He won the European championships in 2000 and has finished third at the world championships on two different occasions.
- The gold medal game in 2006 between Finland and Canada drew a television audience of 5 million in Finland, where curling is not much more than a fringe sport.
- Uusipaavalniemi built his own curling club in his hometown of Hyvinkaa.

SLIDING ALONG

M any curlers may not realize the impact Arnold Asham has had on their games, but the Winnipeg entrepreneur is one of the largest suppliers of curling equipment in the game. Whether it be a slider, a broom, or some clothing, Asham Curling Supplies has touched curlers around the world. A few notes on the man behind the company:

- Asham is a Métis who grew up in Kinosota, Manitoba, and started curling at age 13.
- He started working for the Manitoba Department of Mines and Resources while curling competitively and stumbled upon a material that made for a great slider. He started selling his now famous red-brick sliders out of his basement but when demand took off, he left his government job and went into the curling shoe business full time.

- Asham didn't come up with the original idea for the red-brick slider. A fellow club curler, who worked in the printing business and used this hard plastic material in his work, was the first to put the material on his curling shoe. Asham was attracted by the noise it made and he revolutionized the manner in which it was put on the shoe.
- He sold more than $1 million worth of red-brick sliders.
- He was one of the founders of the World Curling Tour.

His company serves as title sponsor of the circuit.

- He founded a square-dance group called the Asham Stompers, which competed in festivals wearing, of course, Asham curling shoes (without the slider).

- In addition to five kinds of curling shoes, Asham also sells curling brooms, bags, slip-on grippers, gloves, slip-on sliders, and curling apparel.

ALL-IMPORTANT CLUB

The Duddingston Curling Society lays claim to being "the most important curling club in the world." Formed in 1795, the club was the haunt of choice for curlers in Edinburgh, who used the Duddingston loch as their venue. The most distinguished curlers from all over Scotland joined the Duddingston with the fee being three guineas. There were also medals struck, which members wore to "distinguish the members from other gentlemen." There were also rules for the new group, which included a fine for talking politics.

Perhaps the society's main contribution to the game was the establishment of curling's first set of rules. The document, which still exists, is dated January 6, 1804. Many of the rules in that code still exist in some part today, such as No. 10: "A doubtful shot is to be measured by some neutral person whose determination shall be final."

WHAT'S IN A NAME?

Ever wonder how the hog line got its name? According to Scottish curling history, it's a farming term. A hog, in livestock circles, was a name given to a weak member of a litter, a runt, so to speak, specifically with sheep. This hog was more than likely to die before the end of its first year, either at the jaws of a predator or from the farmer who would cull his flock. Similarly, a hogged rock is one that falls short of the line, not making it into play.

CHARACTER GUY

Up until the mid-1950s, curling had been a staid and reserved sport, even at the Canadian championship level. It wasn't considered proper for players to show a lot of emotion or to showboat in any way. But that changed with the arrival of Edmonton's Matt Baldwin. Not only was he a breath of fresh air for fans, he was also a remarkably talented player. Some facts about the three-time Brier winner:

- The first indication that Baldwin was going to buck tradition came in the fifth round of the 1954 Brier in Edmonton. After making his last shot to beat Northern Ontario 6–5 in a close match, Baldwin's third, Glenn Gray, jumped into the air and let out a scream. Baldwin raised a clenched fist and shook it as he came down the ice to celebrate with his team. That night at a banquet, one of the Brier trustees (the or-ganizers of the event) told Baldwin his actions that day weren't acceptable and asked the Alberta skip to keep his emotions in check for the rest of the event.

- Baldwin was one of the first curlers able to slide the entire length of the ice. In the '54 Brier, every time he stepped into the hack, the crowd would yell, "Slide, slide."

- At a major event at Maple Leaf Gardens in Toronto, Baldwin delighted the fans by sliding

Matt Baldwin and Garnet Campbell

the length of the ice with the rock in front of him. Halfway down the sheet, he removed his hand from the stone, nonchalantly rubbed his nose and then replaced his hand on the rock, which was sliding along in front of him, still in position. He stopped the rock perfectly on the button.

- Baldwin became known as a man who never missed a party. After winning the '54 Brier, he went to a party at the host hotel and stayed late. "I just got plastered," he stated of the evening.

- Gunning for his third Brier win in 1957 in Victoria, Baldwin told the media about the host hotel, the Empress, "All those ladies having tea are making so much noise we can't get our rest."

- On the final day of the '57 Brier, Baldwin was suffering so badly from the flu, he brought a chair out onto the backboards and sat in it when his team wasn't shooting

- At the 1971 Brier in Quebec City, a massive blizzard caused a power failure at the arena in the middle of a draw, sending the event into 15 minutes of darkness. When the power came back on the Baldwin team was nowhere to be seen, but on their sheet, all eight rocks were sitting in the four-foot. Baldwin and his team emerged from the bar to where they'd retreated to gales of laughter from the fans. The incident became known as the Baldwin Blackout.

- Baldwin was known as one of the single best shooters in the game. For a number of years, an Edmonton television station conducted a singles competition between some of the top players in the game, Ernie Richardson and Garnett Campbell among them. Baldwin won it six consecutive years, and the station finally had to remove him from the event.

PRESERVED IN GRANITE

The final game of the 1956 Brier is one of the most memorable in the event's history. It required a play-off game (prior to there being regular playoffs) because Ontario and Manitoba tied with identical 8–2 marks. In an extra end of the extra game, Ontario's Alf Phillips appeared to have the match won with a stone 90 percent buried on the button. Billy Walsh of Winnipeg, however, played a perfect come-around tap to score one and win the Brier. So remarkable was the final shot that a fan jumped over the boards, grabbed the winning stone, and disappeared into the crowd. A few weeks later, he presented Walsh with the winning stone mounted on a special plaque to commemorate the fantastic finish.

SUBSTITUTE CHAMPIONS

When the first Brier was held in Toronto in 1927, it was organized late in the curling year, and there was a scramble to assemble the representative teams. Two members of Ontario's team, winners of the Silver Tankard, had to be called back from Florida, where they'd escaped to pass the winter. The team's second, Mel Hunt (father of the late Toronto sportswriter Jim Hunt), and Harry Watson (grandfather of hockey broadcaster Harry Neale) returned with just a few days to spare.

The Nova Scotia entry had its own difficulties. When locals received the invitation to come to Toronto for the first championship, they originally decided to send Murray Macniell's provincial championship rink. But the only one able to make the trip was the skip, so he selected three other skips to join him. The first time the team played together as a team was the opening draw of the Brier. It obviously worked, as the Halifax four became the first Canadian champions.

VISIBLE MINORITY

Only one non-white has won the Canadian men's curling championship. Rudy Ramcharan, who played second for Kevin Martin's winning squad in 1997, is of Guyanese background. He disappeared from curling circles a few years later after trying to run a cash event, officially the World Open but known to many as the Rudy Spiel, with a purse of $500,000. However he was never able to secure the sponsorship, and a number of teams competed and were never fully compensated. Ramcharan became persona non grata among many of the top curlers.

Curling Quote

"There's not too many guys who can really be entrusted with (the ice). Besides, you'd have to be nuts to do it anyway. The hours, the work, the stress, the pressure of it all and I don't even get to curl on it. I'm the only one held responsible. It doesn't matter if the rocks are no good, or if the weather is bad, in the end, it all reflects on me.

So come on curling gods, keep taking care of me."

—Icemaker Dave Merklinger, who made the ice for the 2007 Tim Hortons Brier in Hamilton, as told to the *Hamilton Spectator*

CLOSE TO PERFECTION

There has never been an eight-ender in Brier history, but there have been two occasions when it seemed almost certain the perfect end would be recorded.

- In 1947 Jimmy Welsh of Manitoba played Prince Edward Island's Frank Acorn. In the eighth end, Acorn was looking at seven Manitoba counters, and his final rock was light, stopping just into the twelve-foot. Welsh needed to be better than that Prince Edward Island rock to score the magical eight, but he was heavy and ended up scoring seven.

- In the 1936 Brier, Ken Watson's team was rolling to win after win, and in its seventh match it faced a winless Prince Edward Island squad. Prior to the game, Watson gave lead Charlie Kerr a cigar, which Kerr smoked as the game progressed. In the first end, with Watson sitting five, third Grant Watson threw a draw that appeared to be perfect but just a little light. Kerr and second Marvin McIntyre put the brooms to it and just as it approached the rings, an ash from the cigar dropped in front of the stone, and it ground to an immediate halt, inches from the target. When the next two Manitoba stones found the house, the team had a seven-ender that could have been eight were it not for the cigar ash.

A HEART OF PURPLE

The Purple Heart is a highly sought-after crest for male curlers in Canada. It signifies participation in the Brier and a provincial champion. Curlers who have one can thank a team from Ontario for that honour.

For the first six years of the Canadian championship, Purple Heart crests were not awarded. Each curler did receive a small pin.

At the seventh championship, Gordon Campbell and his rink from the Hamilton Thistle Curling Club arrived at the championship with lavish crests presented to them by the Ontario Curling Association proclaiming them to be Ontario champions. Senator Jack Haig of Winnipeg, who was one of the Brier trustees (essentially the organizers) noticed the crests and asked Campbell about them. "I think we should do something like that," he said.

The next year, every participant received the famous heart-shaped crest. However the original ones were not purple, but red. The colour changed in 1940 and has remained purple ever since.

TANKARD TIME

The trophy presented to the winner of the Brier is known as the Macdonald Brier Tankard and has a long history, somewhat longer than the championship itself. It was not even created for the Brier but for the Manitoba Bonspiel where it was first awarded to the winner in 1925. Presented by Macdonald Tobacco, the cup itself was hand-tooled in Great Britain.

In 1927, however, Macdonald Tobacco, the sponsor of the Brier, elected to use the trophy for the new national championship. It remained the official trophy until 1979, when the tobacco company ended its sponsorship.

For the first 27 years of the Brier, the names of the four winners were engraved into a heart-shaped crest and affixed to a base. However, after that period, there was no room left, and the players' names were put onto a single plaque on the back of the trophy.

When Labatt took over sponsorship in 1980, it brought in its own trophy, which was presented until 2000. At that time, Nokia assumed title sponsorship, and in consultation with the Canadian Curling Association, had the original Macdonald Tankard reinstated. It was upgraded to the tune of $10,000 and, with the addition of a series of new base levels, every winning team from 1927 onward had their names engraved onto a heart-shaped crest.

Curling Quote

"A match for money even though the sum be devoted to charity, would drag down curling to the level of baseball."

—A director of the Grand National Curling Club (forerunner of the United States Curling Association) in response to an 1870 challenge from Scottish curler Sir William Elliot, who said he'd play any North American team for £500 sterling

SPONSORS

Curling has had a number of interesting sponsors over the years, and in comparison to many other sports, the sponsors have stayed for extended periods of time. Here's a list of some of the leading sponsors of major events, and the length of their support:

Canadian Men's

Macdonald Tobacco	50 years
Labatt	20 years
Nokia	4 years
Tim Hortons	4 years*

World Championship

Scotch Whiskey Company	9 years
Air Canada	18 years
Safeway	2 years
Ford	14 years*
No sponsor	5 years

Canadian Women's

Dominion Grocery	7 years
Macdonald Tobacco	8 years
Scott Paper (later Kruger)	27 years*
No sponsor	6 years

*on going

BATTLE OF THE SEXES

As long as male and female curlers have been throwing rocks, a war has been waged as to which sex is the better at curling. Over the years, there have been a number of highly publicized battles of the sexes. Here are a few notables:

- In November 1972, Vera Pezer and her team of Canadian champions challenged reigning men's Canadian and world champion Orest Meleschuk to a game, one that eventually found its way onto the CBC. Pezer ended up winning the game 4–3 when Meleschuk missed his last shot of the game. The announcers, Don Chevrier and Don Duguid, summed up Meleschuk's sentiments:

    Chevrier: "I'm not sure Meleschuck can really believe it."

    Duguid: "He'll believe it tomorrow morning, Don."

- In October 2005, multiple-Brier winner Randy Ferbey and his team took on Jennifer Jones, the reigning Canadian women's champion, in a skins-format gender battle. The game was broadcast across Canada on Sportsnet, and what viewers saw was a Ferbey domination. He won seven of the eight available skins.

SCIENCE OF CURLING

Why a curling rock actually curls has been a mystery to many curlers, but the CBC radio program *Quirks and Quarks* tried to de-mystify it during a 1980 broadcast. Here, according to Dr. Mark Shegelski, are the reasons a 40-pound piece of granite curls.

When a rock is turning as it travels down the ice, one side is turning toward the direction the rock is travelling and the other away from it.

The speed of the two edges relative to the ice is different due to friction. When a rock is first thrown, the amount of friction is about the same. But as the rock slows, the edge that is turning back toward the curler (the right side on an in-turn) is turning more slowly because it is turning in the opposite direction to which the rock is travelling.

Because this side is turning slower, friction has a greater effect upon it. That causes the stone to deflect to one side (in the case of the in-turn, to the right).

The sharpest move a rock makes is often right at the end as it stops, because one side of the rock stops first while the other side continues to rotate.

And now you know!

REGAL CURLING

Frederick Hamilton-Temple-Blackwood, first Earl of Dufferin, first Marquess of Dufferin and Ava—the name may not mean much to curlers, but this gentleman served as Governor General of Canada from 1872 to 1878 and had a profound effect upon the sport of curling.

A devoted enthusiast of the roaring game, in 1873, at his own expense, he added a curling rink to Rideau Hall, the Governor General's official residence. It exists to this day, along with the Governor General's Club, an exclusive and honorary club whose membership is made up of those who have given a great deal to the sport of curling.

And he presented a trophy for annual competition, which came to be known simply as "the Governor General's." It was awarded to the winners of the Ontario double-rink competition, and for many years was emblematic of the provincial championship. The competition ceased being held in 1996.

WOMEN'S DATES

A few notable dates in women's curling:

- The first women's curling club in Canada was established in 1894 in Montreal. Prior to that, women were discouraged from coming to curling competitions due to liquor being present.
- The Ladies Curling Association of the Canadian Branch of the Royal Caledonian Curling Club, which became the governing body for women's curling, was established in 1904. It looked after the rules and competitions for the women's game in the Quebec and Ontario regions, although there were few formal events held.
- The Canadian Ladies Curling Association was formed in 1960 (taking over authority from the above-mentioned body), and a year later, the first Canadian women's curling championship was held. Prior to the event, Dominion Stores, a nationwide chain of grocery stores, approached the fledgling association and asked if it could be the title sponsor, one of the few times a sponsor has come to the event and solicited involvement and not the other way around.
- The United States Women's Curling Association has a longer history, having formed in 1947. The first national women's championship was held in 1949, although it wasn't until 1977 that it was formally recognized as the national championship. Prior to that, it was run as a bonspiel.
- The first women's world championship was held in 1979 in Perth, Scotland, sponsored by the Royal Bank of Scotland.

JUNIOR-SENIOR

Only eight male curlers have won both the Canadian Junior and the Canadian Men's championship. Here is the list, noting the first time they won each event:

Name	Junior	Men's
Ed Lukowich	1962	1978
Neil Houston	1975	1986
Kevin Martin	1985	1991
Dan Petryk	1985	1991
Jon Mead	1986	1999
Scott Pfeifer	1994	2001
Craig Savill	1988	2007
Brent Laing	1988	2007

BAD ICE

Icemaking has become a combination of art and science, and it's not often these days that curlers at major championships have to suffer with poor conditions. That hasn't always been the case, however. Following are some recent examples of horrible ice at significant events.

1970 Brier

The ice at this championship was so heavy it removed almost all shotmaking abilities. Instead, players just heaved the rocks down the ice as hard as they could and hoped they'd make the rings. In one memorable game, British Columbia's Lyle Dagg came short of the rings with his last rock to lose to Ontario's Paul Savage. Dagg was playing a hit.

1992 Olympics

Curling was a demonstration sport at the '92 Games. The competition was held in the ice rink of Pralognan-la-Vanoise, a venue about 50 kilometres from the host city, Albertville. Right from the start, the refrigeration unit didn't work properly, and only one of the four sheets in the facility froze properly. The two middle sheets were unplayable and were covered with carpet, so the entire competition was reduced to two sheets. One was extremely frosty and the other always had a small film of water on it. The icemakers called in Canadian skip Kevin Martin, who had icemaking experience, to try to help, but when the opposing teams learned he was involved, they protested, and Martin was forbidden from helping. At the end of the week, Martin had the highest percentage of any curler at a ridiculously low 63, the lowest winning mark of any international championship on record.

1981 World Curling Championships

In the final game between the United States and Switzerland, the ice plant at Thompson arena failed in the late ends, and the ice began to melt slowly. By the time the teams played the final end, a small layer of water covered the surface, making it almost impossible to get rocks in play. The U.S. team hogged its first four shots, and Switzerland went on to win the title by a score of 2–1.

2001 Brier

When players complained that the ice conditions were too straight, preventing any aggressive play, the Canadian Curling Association asked renowned icemaker Shorty Jenkins to come in and work his magic. Despite his reputation for making superb ice, he had never worked on the Brier ice before. However, with limited time and resources, Jenkins overdid it, and put too much curl onto the sheets, making it nearly impossible to play. Following two draws, the CCA returned to its existing icemaker and flooded the surface to start over.

2005 Women's World Championship

The event was held at the Lagoon Leisure Centre in Paisley, Scotland, and icemakers had their work cut out for them at this global tilt thanks to a number of factors. First, the ice rink was located next to a swimming pool, and humidity—curling ice's worst enemy—was a constant factor. Also, because organizers refused to pay for a deionizer for the water that was used to pebble the ice, the first few draws had horrid conditions. Finally, the arena floor was concave, so the outside sheets were thicker ice than the inside ones, meaning significant differences in conditions between each sheet. Conditions were so bad, the fourth draw was actually cancelled. The event was also marred by officials who walked out after they learned they weren't going to be paid, and by low attendance—often times there were more people on the ice than in the stands.

ORIGINAL OLSON

A lot of curlers have stepped on the name Olson over the years, and that's just fine with the family. Olson, you see, is synonymous with hacks, and for many years, the company that bears the name of the inventor made a majority of the toeholds in use across the world.

Elias Bjarni "Ole" Olson was the inventor of the rubber hack. Patented in 1939, it was the standard for almost 50 years. (Some are still in use today, although a newer model—the Marco hack—has taken over.)

Olson came up with his idea while playing in a bonspiel in Saskatoon. During a crucial time in the game, Olson went to play a shot, and his foot slipped, causing him to miss. At that time, hacks were merely holes chipped out of the ice. On his way home from that bonspiel, he stopped at a tire company and purchased some raw rubber with which he began to experiment, moulding it into different shapes before arriving at the final product. So successful was his invention that he was swamped by orders from curling clubs around the world.

Olson was also the first person to use paint on curling ice to distinguish the house, that coming in 1926, and he also invented a curling rink ice shaver as an inexpensive alternative to the Zamboni. Among his other inventions are a pebbling can and a rock measure.

Olson passed away in 1964 and was posthumously inducted into the Canadian Curling Hall of Fame in 2000.

HISTORY ON DISPLAY

D on and Elva Turner enjoyed collecting all things curling. In fact, they liked it so much they turned their basement into a museum to house all their wares. The artifacts the couple assembled are thought to be the largest collection of curling memorabilia in the world.

The collection began in 1974 when Elva curled in the Canadian Seniors in Halifax and returned home to Weyburn, Saskatchewan, with a small collection of pins and some curling photos. From there, the collecting became voracious and soon the couple's basement was turned into a museum. School groups and avid curlers used to come by to see the displays.

That was great for a while, but eventually the collection outgrew their home. That's when their home city of Weyburn stepped up and allowed them to create the Turner Curling Museum in a 2,600-square-foot building attached to the city's recreation centre. The operation is the world's first curling museum.

Inside, visitors see rarities such as a set of circular curling irons with iron handles, used in the late 1800s in the Ottawa Valley. There is also an early rock sharpener used by the Queen City Curling Stone Co. of Regina in the 1930s. A prized possession is a pair of rocks awarded as a prize in the 1927 Brier, the first Canadian championship.

But undoubtedly the most impressive display is the massive collection of pins, collected through years and years of attending major curling events, especially the world championship. It's estimated there are 18,000 curling pins, and no one is quite sure if that is the largest collection in the world, but it is certainly impressive.

Don Turner passed away in 2006, and Elva maintains the museum.

CURLING IN THE BIBLE?

At the opening banquet for the 1966 Brier in Halifax, the speaker, Dr. J.B. Hardie, a professor at Pine Hill Divinity College, light-heartedly suggested that curling must have been around for a lot longer than originally thought. To back up this point, he gave a number of examples of curling being mentioned in the Bible. First he said that the purest of curlers must be the leads: "He that is without sin among you, let him cast the first stone" (John 8:7).

Then he said there were a great many talented curlers back in the Holy Land: "Among all this people, there were seven hundred chosen men left-handed; every one could sling stones at an hair breadth, and not miss" (Judges 20:16).

Finally, he argued, there's nothing like the Canadian men's championship: "He that is best among them, is as a brier" (Micah 7:4).

LATE NIGHT CURLING

Curling made it to late-night television in 2002 during its play at the Olympics in Salt Lake City, Utah. That's when the titans of American talks shows—Jay Leno and David Letterman—made light of the cult hit. Leno had a joke about it during his opening monologue on February 19, 2002, saying: "Did you see the curling today? Pretty exciting. The gold medal ended up going to a Brazilian cleaning team."

Letterman used curling as a theme for one of his famous Top 10 lists. It was titled: "10 Ways to Make Curling More Exciting."

10. How about calling it anything but curling?

9. Instead of weird lookin' Norwegian dudes in sweaters—babes in lingerie.

8. Only allow French judges.

7. Sweep the stone toward the hog line and then…okay, I don't know crap about curling.

6. Is it too much to ask for one curler to bite another curler?

5. Throw in one of them miniature-golf windmills.

4. Instead of a granite stone, use the frozen head of Walt Disney.

3. 40% of final score comes from the swimsuit competition.

2. You don't think curling is exciting? What are you, insane?

1. First place gets gold medal, the rest are sent to Camp X-Ray.

CURLING ART

There are a number of remarkable curling paintings around the world, but few that match the impressiveness of Charles Lees' work of the Grand Match that took place January 25, 1848. Titled "The Grand Match at Linlithgow Loch," it shows what appears to be a wild game of curling with men in top hats and full dress. According to historian Bob Cowan, the curling was between 35 teams from the north and 35 from the south. Reportedly, 6,000 people were present. The painting of this event showed only a small number of these folks, and many notables of Scottish curling are represented. In fact, Cowan stated, there is evidence to suggest that Lees travelled to the homes of curlers to sketch them. The painting was completed in 1849, and the Royal Caledonian Curling Club purchased it in 1898. For many years, it hung in the curling club at Perth. In 2006, Sotheby's appraised the work at £500,000. The work now hangs in the Scottish National Portrait Gallery in Edinburgh.

TV PAY DAY

The TSN Skins Game is an innovative, made-for-television event that was developed at a time when curling was suffering from plenty of low-scoring, defensive play that left audiences snoring. It not only became one of the most popular curling events for viewers, but also one of the most lucrative for curlers. A few notes about the skins:

Ed Werenich and Russ Howard

- The idea for the format was developed by Jim Thompson, then vice-president of TSN, and entrepreneur Doug Maxwell. They decided to break all the rules in building a new event that would sell to television audiences.
- The event has been held in all ten provinces as well as the Yukon.
- McCain Foods sponsored the tournament from 1989 to 2004, then it went dormant until 2007, when it was revived and held at Ontario's Casino Rama.

- The highest payout for a single skins game came in 2004 when Kevin Martin earned $100,500.
- Wayne Middaugh has been a member of seven winning teams and has earned a total of $365,750 in his skins game appearances.
- A women's version of the skins game was held for eight years but dropped in 2003.

CURLER STATS

Who are curlers? If they live in Canada, there's a pretty good idea of their profile, demographically speaking, thanks to the Print Measurement Bureau, a research organization aimed at the print media.

Here's who the Canadian Curler is as of 2006:

- one of 754,000 Canadians
- 55 per cent are male
- between the ages of 35 and 49
- lives in a community between 500,000 and one million residents
- lives in a rural prairie location
- 20 per cent have a university degree
- had an annual household income between $75,000 and $99,000
- 49 per cent engage in volunteer activities
- a majority also golfed or fished

CURLING IN TELEVISION COMMERCIALS

Curling has appeared numerous times in commercials, being used to sell everything from beer to cellphones. Here are some of the more memorable commercials.

Advertiser: Cialis (a drug for erectile dysfunction)

A man is shown delivering a stone, and in doing so falls and appears to be injured. His wife comes to comfort him, and he announces that he'd better quit because of the injury. The next scene shows the couple leaving the club for their car, and the woman confronts her husband about his "injury," which appears to have suddenly healed. A large Cialis logo then appears.

Advertiser: Labatt Beer

A snowy street scene is the opening shot of this commercial, with a hot dog cart as the central feature. The operator of the cart is putting it into place for the day and drops a bag of buns. When he bends down to pick them up, he lets go of the cart, which starts to slide down the street, turning like a curling rock. Suddenly, people appear from everywhere, from their porches, from shovelling their driveways, from taxis, all with brooms, and begin sweeping the hot dog cart as if it's the shot to win the Brier. The vendor is barking out orders like a skip, and after encouraging the group to sweep, suddenly bellows at them to stop. The cart slowly stops sliding just before hitting a postal truck, and a close-up shows the mustard container rubbing part of the truck, wobbling, but not falling over. As the cart comes to a stop, there is a spontaneous cheer from the group.

Advertiser: Scotties tissues

A woman is shopping and places a box of Scotties tissues in her cart. As she walks forward with her cart, two women appear, one with a corn broom, the other with a push broom. They sweep the cart toward the cash register, stopping once, then restarting and concluding when the cart reaches its destination. They look at each other and nod in satisfaction. A voiceover states: "Scotties, proud sponsor of women's curling for over 25 years."

Advertiser: Office Depot

An advertisement that aired in the United States prior to the 2002 Olympics showed a man in what appears to be a lounge, watching television. A close-up of a rock being swept appears on the screen, and the obviously confused man says: "What is that?" The screen then shows the words "But, if life was like Office Depot…" The same scene is repeated, only this time, U.S. curler Don Barcome responds to the man's question by placing a curling rock on the table in front of him and saying: "Curling, an ancient Scottish ice sport played with a 42-pound stone." The scene then cuts to an Office Depot store, where an announcer says: "If you want expert answers whenever you need them, come to Office Depot." At the end of the commercial, a tag points out that the retailer is a sponsor of the U.S. Olympic team.

ROCK BOTTOM

There are curling rocks in unusual places but perhaps none stranger than the several crates of stones that rest at the bottom of the Atlantic Ocean, somewhere off the coast of Newfoundland. How did they end up there? According to Doug Maxwell in *Canada Curls*, in the early 1800s there was a challenge issued by a group of Scottish soldiers stationed at Long-Sault to a group of Scottish expats living in Lachute, Quebec. The difficulty was that there were not enough curling rocks to hold such a match and so an order was put in to the homeland to ship 16 to Quebec. Unfortunately, the ship carrying the rocks sank off the Grand Banks, dropping the bits of Ailsa Craig granite to the bottom of the ocean.

DEADLY BUSINESS

Curling has played a small role in two tragic and notable events. The first was on April 30, 1912, 20 days after the sinking of the Titanic. On April 17, the Mackay-Bennett set sail from Halifax with the grim job of recovering bodies from the sinking of the ocean liner. Over the course of the next few days, men on the ship pulled in 306 bodies and after sailing home, delivered them to the Mayflower Curling Club, which served as the morgue. While the ship was at sea, coffins had been piled high at the club awaiting the grim arrival.

The second event was on December 21, 1988, when Pan Am Flight 103 was destroyed by a bomb over Lockerbie, Scotland. Many parts of the plane fell on the town, and the first medical officer on the scene was Dr. Graeme Adam. Just a few weeks earlier, Adam had won the Scottish men's curling championship and was soon to leave for the world championships in Milwaukee, Wisconsin. But his practice time was cut short for two reasons. First, he was busy dealing with the accident, and second, as in Halifax, the local curling club was transformed into a morgue to house the bodies of those killed in the crash. The curling ice was understandably not available for curling.

Adam went on to finish with a 5–4 record at the world final.

PURPLE RAGE

Curling has a great deal of tradition, and as one organization found out, curlers don't want to lose that.

In 1980, when Labatt took over sponsorship of the Brier from Macdonald Tobacco, it decided to create a new crest to present to all participants. This was a replacement for the famed Purple Heart.

"We weren't really keen on keeping the Purple Heart," admitted Dick Bradbeer, head of marketing for Labatt at the time. "We wanted something more Labatt-oriented."

In place of the heart was an oval-shaped crest that had images of the Purple Heart and the Macdonald Brier Tankard, the trophy that was presented to the winning team up until Labatt replaced it with its own tankard. Among the curlers, it became known as the Doily.

But curlers from coast to coast—those who had played in the Brier and those who had merely watched it—were enraged. How could this new sponsor replace the historic crest? There were petitions and plenty of media attention on the issue of a crest. A front-page editorial in the *Ontario Curling Report* admonishing Labatt for the change. It read:

The Heart is symbolic of the Brier; it represents curling supremacy. After the Brier, all that remains are the fine memories and the Heart.

Every competitive male curler dreams of playing in the Brier. The Brier is the pot of gold at the end of the rainbow. The Brier is the Stanley Cup, the Super Bowl, the end all, be all.

Now the new sponsors of the Brier have created a new symbol that they are incorporating into a crest. The new crest does not resemble the Heart, although they have tried to keep the coveted Heart by placing its design in the centre of this new symbol. This new creation destroys the image that has been established from 50 years of annual competition. Every curler in Canada identifies with the Purple Heart; it is the symbol of excellence.

Labatt's sponsorship is a welcome addition to the game. However, curling has established legends built around the Heart. You can do anything with the design of the Heart but don't mess with the winner, the Heart of the game.

The paper was the final straw. "When we saw that newspaper, we realized just how important the Purple Heart was," said Bradbeer. "It wasn't that we were being stubborn, it was another case of not realizing the importance the curlers put on it."

Labatt reissued the crest in the famous shape and colour to the delight of all. All the players from the 1980 Brier—the first sponsored by Labatt—ended up with two crests: the Purple Heart and the Doily, now a rare collector's item.

Curling Quote

"His sister said the car looked like it had hit a moose. So I guess John is built like a moose."

—Kevin Martin on his third, John Morris, who was hit by a car just days before the start of the 2007 Tim Hortons Brier

AMERICAN SUCCESS

Bob Nichols and Bill Strum have won more World Curling Championships than any other Americans, with three wins to their credit. That's quite an achievement considering the U.S.A. has won the world title just four times.

THE MANITOBA BONSPIEL

The Manitoba Bonspiel, also known as the MCA after the Manitoba Curling Association, which runs the event, dates back to 1884 when the first bonspiel in Winnipeg was held. There were 65 teams from all over the province at that first event, which led to the formal start to the Manitoba Bonspiel, which began five years later and continues to this day. Notes about the famed event:

- In the early days, the event became so popular that for several years, the sitting of the Manitoba Legislature was cancelled due to the inability to get a quorum; so many members were on the ice.
- In 1988, to celebrate the bonspiel's centennial, an all-out effort to attract teams produced the largest field ever for a curling event—1,280 teams.
- The event is open to all teams of male curlers, and there are regular entrants from across Canada, the United States, Europe, and Asia.
- Entries into the provincial championship are awarded to the top finishers in the bonspiel.
- In recent years, the number of teams in the bonspiel has dropped and there was discussion about allowing women to enter but that was never passed by organizers.
- Even with the drop in teams, the Manitoba Bonspiel remains the largest curling bonspiel in the world.

A SPIKED TROPHY

In 1902–03, the first visit by a group of Scottish curlers to Canada took place, with the Scots playing a lengthy string of games that took them from Halifax to Winnipeg, with stops at most major cities in between. Such a success was the tour that in 1909, a group of Canadian curlers went the other way.

With the event becoming a friendly rivalry of significance, it began to catch the attention of a great many curling enthusiasts, including Donald Smith, Lord Strathcona and Mount Royal. Smith spent his early years in Canada, working with the Hudson's Bay Company, eventually becoming the president of the firm. He also was a Member of Parliament and was a founding member of the Canadian Pacific Railway, becoming such an important figure in that operation that when the transcontinental railroad was being completed, Smith was selected to drive the last spike.

Smith returned to Great Britain in his later years to take his spot in the House of Lords. He so loved both continents and the game of curling that he decided to present a trophy for regular competition between the two sides of touring curlers. Thus, in 1909, the Canadian team was the first to win the Strathcona Cup.

Today the Scots travel to Canada in years that end in a three, while the Canadians go the other way in years that end in an eight. The trophy used to make the transatlantic trip with the defending champions, but now is considered so valuable that it resides permanently in Scotland.

NORTHERN AFFAIR

Every team in the Brier represents a single province or territory, with the exception of Northern Ontario. The reason it has a spot in the field is history and respect. While the definitive answer to its inclusion is unknown (some say the size of the province and the overall population necessitated two entries), when the first Brier was held in 1927, it is believed a rink from Northern Ontario was invited by Brier organizers to make the field an even number. Although two other teams—Montreal and Toronto—were removed from the invitation list in 1931, Northern Ontario remains.

When asked why Northern Ontario stayed in the field, David M. Stewart, head of the Macdonald Tobacco Company, said, "When you invite someone into your living room, you don't invite them to leave just because the numbers aren't right."

STONES OF A DIFFERENT MATERIAL

It's rare today to see a curling stone made of something other than granite, but in the early days of the sport, when rocks were difficult to come by, ardent players used almost anything they could get their hands on to play their favourite sport. Here are a few examples:

- **Cannonballs:** this story has never been conclusively proven, but as the story goes, in the late 1700s, British soldiers melted down cannonballs and used them to curl on the Plains of Abraham.
- **Jam cans:** in western Canada, schoolchildren who were too small to play with the 42-pound granite stones used jam can "rocks" —cans that were filled with rocks or cement with a piece of wire or other material stuck into them for a handle.
- **Thunder mugs:** in some spots on the Prairies, thunder mugs (yes, those bedpans from days gone by) were, like jam cans, filled with granite and used for playing pieces.
- **Irons:** perhaps a derivative of the cannonballs, iron "stones" were, as the name suggests, made of iron and about a third the size of a traditional curling rock. Their weight made it next to impossible to play takeouts. Irons were used prominently in Quebec and eastern Ontario.

- **Wooden stones:** plugs of wood—sometimes off the end of telephone poles—were used to provide lightweight stones for young people. They were also utilized in areas where curlers were unable to afford regular rocks.
- **Little rocks**: Developed in the 1990s, smaller versions of regular rocks made of plastic appeared in curling rinks across Canada. These allowed children as young as five to start playing, and resulted in a huge boom of pint-sized players.

This pint-sized curler is lining up a shot with a Little Rock, a scaled-down version of traditional granite stones.

TIME TO CURL

Most sports have time clocks, which tick off the amount of time for the game to be contested. In curling, however, for the longest time (excuse the pun) there was no such thing. Games lasted as long as they lasted. Some contests at major championships stretched to four hours. In one memorable Ontario provincial championship in the 1980s, an evening draw had to be delayed because a game from the afternoon draw was nearing its fifth hour.

In 1983, curling entrepreneur Doug Maxwell came up with the idea of a time limit for curling, but to make it fair, he decided each team should be timed independently. To test out his theory, he purchased a chess time clock and sat behind the ice at competitive games in the Toronto area. Each team was timed for how long it took them to play.

Time clocks were introduced to competitive play at the 1986 TSN Skins Game, and the result was dramatic— teams played to their limits, not wasting any time, especially in the early parts of an end when strategy decisions were less involved.

A few years later, organizers of the 1989 World Curling Championships in Milwaukee were dealing with a time problem. The International Curling Federation integrated the men's and women's championships into one event, meaning four draws a day. In order to make this work and avoid curling around the clock, they elected to implement Maxwell's time clocks, giving each team a specified amount of time to complete their game. The results were a success and most other jurisdictions soon followed, adding time clocks to their championships.

Today, time clocks are a regular part of every major curling event.

ON THE TUBE

The first televised coverage of the Brier was in 1962, when, thanks to a last-minute okay from network executives, the CBC drove its cameras and trucks to Kitchener, Ontario, to cover the playoff game between Saskatchewan's Ernie Richardson and Hec Gervais of Alberta.

Regularly scheduled coverage of the final draw started in 1973, and it didn't have a great beginning. In the era before playoffs, Harvey Mazinke's team from Saskatchewan played so well that the final draw of the round robin—the one the CBC came to cover—was meaningless; Mazinke won the title the previous evening.

CURLING ROYALTY

Two curlers of some note have gone from the ice to the viceregal's chair. Errik Willis was part of a curling team that competed for Canada at the 1932 Olympic Games in Lake Placid, New York, where curling was a demonstration sport. On January 15, 1960, he was appointed Lieutenant-Governor of Manitoba, holding the office for a term of five years.

In 1986 Sylvia Fedoruk became Saskatchewan's Lieutenant-Governor, a role she kept until 1989. On the ice, Fedoruk was also a member of the team skipped by Joyce Potter that captured the first Canadian women's championship in 1961.

THE LONG AND THE SHORT(ER) OF IT

At the semi-annual meeting of the Ontario Curling Association in 1906, officials passed a regulation changing the length of competitive games from 22 ends to 18.

TIMELINE OF
THE FREE-GUARD ZONE

The free-guard zone is regarded by many as a rule that saved championship curling. The rule allows for plenty of offence and lots of rocks in play, meaning scoring. That makes the game appealing for fans both at venues and watching on television. Prior to its introduction, curling was a defence game with low scores. Here is a timeline of how the rule came to be:

1986: Russ and Glenn Howard develop a method of practice that is essentially a one-on-one game that doesn't allow takeouts on rocks unless they are in the rings.

1991: Organizers of the Moncton 100, a lucrative bonspiel held to celebrate the centennial of the New Brunswick city, utilize what is known as the Howard Rule—the first four rocks of any end cannot be removed regardless of where they come to rest.

1992: A modified version of the Howard Rule, dubbed the free-guard zone, is used at the Olympics. It states that any of the first four rocks of an end that come to rest in front of the tee line and outside of the rings may not be removed. The World Curling Federation adopts the same rule for play in all international championships including the world final. Every member country of the WCF adopts the rule for national play, with the exception of Canada. The Canadian Curling Association elects to remain with the traditional rules and study the free-guard zone for two years.

1993: Ontario becomes the first jurisdiction in Canada to change its rules, adopting a modified version of the free-guard zone, limiting it to the first three rocks of any end for its provincial finals. Russ Howard wins the Ontario, Canadian, and world championships using three different rules: three-rock free-guard zone at the Ontario final; no free-guard zone at the Canadian; four-rock free-guard zone at the world championship.

1994: The Canadian Curling Association adopts a trial of the three-rock free-guard zone rule beginning with its 1994 national championships. It continues with the rule for almost a decade.

2003: The CCA finally falls into line with the rest of the curling world and changes to the four-rock free-guard zone beginning with the 2004 championships. The Canadian Mixed becomes the first event in that country to use the four-rock rule.

ELECTRONIC EYE

In 1986, the Canadian Curling Association institut-
ed curling's equivalent of line judges, placing officials
on the hog line to call infractions at the men's and wom-
en's national championships. The umpires were situated
at either side of the hog line, and if both confirmed that
a player failed to clearly release the stone before the hog
line, the rock was removed from play.

The decision was not popular with all curlers, and
over the course of the next 17 years there were many
charges of incorrect calls, some which cost teams
championships.

That all came to an end in 2003 when something
known as Eye on the Hog was put in place. This system
was a series of sensors, one in the ice and one in the rock.
If a player failed to release the rock before it
reached the hog line, a red light on the handle flashed. If the player released the
rock before the hog line, a green
light went on.

The technological advancement
not only ended all arguments about
human error, but removed the cost
of having numerous extra officials at
the event.

CURLING, ETCETERA

159

TAKEN FOR GRANITE

Curlers might not think in too much detail about the material in the rocks they throw up and down the ice, but the granite used in curling rocks is very important. Over the years, there have been many different types of granite tried in curling stones, including Canadian granite as well as some from India.

But the best continues to be from Scotland and Wales. For many years, the best granite came from the Scottish island of Ailsa Craig, but quarrying there is no longer allowed. Almost all of the granite used to produce today's curling rocks comes from Garn For Quarry in northwest Wales.

According to the Canada Curling Stone Company, here is a list of the various types of granite used in curling rocks currently in play around the world:

- **blue hone:** light grey in colour with random white specks. Often has half-moon shaped chips in the strike band.
- **red/brown trefor:** light to dark reddish brown marked by larger grains with white and black flecks.
- **blue trefor:** bluish-grey in colour with white and black flecks. It's prone to premature pitting.
- **grey trefor:** greyish brown in colour, also with white and black flecks throughout.

- **keanie:** pinkish in colour with large white spots and black flecks throughout.
- **common green Ailsa Craig:** greenish in colour with large black flecks that usually have white deposits around them.

GIVING UP

Conceding a game at the Canadian championship is an accepted practice these days. When one team feels it no longer has a chance to win, it can elect to quit. But that wasn't always the case. Prior to the 1973 Brier, teams were required to complete all 12 ends, no matter the score.

A BLIND EYE

I t's not unusual for individuals to take up curling when they retire, and that's just what Ray Kotanen of Thunder Bay, Ontario, did in 1991 when he turned 65.

Kotanen joined the Ezyduzit Curling League for retired men and proved to be not only enthusiastic but also a quick learner. However, he did have one limitation—he couldn't see the other end of the ice, his skip, or his skip's broom. Diabetes robbed him of vision in his right eye and left him with limited sight in his left. Kotanen relied on verbal instructions relayed to him by the sweepers and managed to become quite proficient. Still, he disliked being dependant on others.

All that changed when friend Ray Paju decided to help out. Paju developed a high-intensity strobe light that fastened onto the handle of Kotanen's skips' broom. The light blinked a strong signal from the skip's end of the ice and was visible for Kotanen sitting in the hack. He no longer needed the verbal instructions—he could see just fine. Another example of ingenuity allowing a curler to play the game he loves.

RECORD-SETTING CURLING

Camille Villeneuve of Chicoutimi, Quebec, is a guy who has trouble playing on a regular team. For that matter, he has trouble finding a steady club. But that's something he planned. Since 2005, Villeneuve has ventured across Canada and the United States playing in as many different curling clubs with as many different teammates as possible. He travels by camper, setting up games ahead of time often playing two or three a night. To date, he's competed at more than 611 clubs and played with more than 1,800 different teammates. Both marks are recognized in the *Guinness Book of World Records*. All of his adventures came late in life for Villeneuve. At the age of 79 years old, he's still going, hoping to reach 700 clubs by his 80th birthday.

Curling Quote

"I'm actually looking forward to playing in a country where five feet (tall) might actually be the average."

—The diminutive Kelly Scott on playing the world championship in Japan in 2007

AGE-OLD ROCKERS

Curling is known as a game for all ages, and certainly that's proven to be the case over the long history of the sport. Here are a few examples of "elderly" competitors, elderly being a relative term:

- At age 50 Russ Howard became the oldest person to win a gold medal at the 2006 Olympic Games, capturing the medal for Canada.
- At age 55, Bud Somerville played for the U.S. team at the 1992 Olympics.
- At 94, Einer Egilssen plays three times a week in Woodstock, Ontario. He's played the game for 60 years.
- At 99, Jack Grossart played twice a week in Weston, Ontario.
- Jack Watkins, at 93, has a certificate from the Guinness Book of World Records, stating he is the oldest living curler. He plays twice a week in Sudbury, Ontario.
- In Regina, Phil Ward competed regularly at the Tartan Curling Club at the age of 102.

DOUBLING UP

Doubles, in sporting terms, usually conjures up images of tennis, where teams of two players take on similar teams.

But doubles is also now a part of curling—mixed doubles, to be more precise, with teams comprised of one man and one woman, just as in tennis. The format had its genesis in another event, the Continental Cup, where teams representing North America and Europe compete in various formats, one of which is mixed doubles.

Each end of mixed doubles begins with a rock sitting behind the button guarded by a stone in front of the rings. Each team delivers five shots, and the teams can decide which team member throws first, allowing any order on any given end. The player that throws the first stone of the end also throws the last one, with the other player delivering the middle three rocks.

Hoping to get at least one more discipline added to the curling program at the Olympics, the World Curling Federation promoted mixed doubles as a stand-alone event. It even created a separate world championship, with the first one held in Vierumaki, Finland, in March 2008.

PIN MOGUL

Curling pins have a long association with the sport, with clubs, events and even people producing their own unique ones. Because there are thousands and thousands of different pins, collecting them has become a passionate pastime for many, much like collecting baseball cards would be for a fan of that game.

Go to any big curling event and you're sure to see pin collectors, both those who do the job seriously and put out massive displays, and others who are just trying to pick up a few while at the bonspiel or championship.

No matter what the level of interest, all these folks can thank one Saskatchewan resident for most of their fun. Laurie Artiss has become one of the world's largest makers of pins, and it all started thanks to his love of curling.

Artiss started his association with curling in 1962, covering the Brier for the *Brandon Sun*. He moved to Regina in the late 1960s to take a job as a sports writer with the *Regina Leader-Post*, and in 1970 he started a curling supply business. Around that time, he grew frustrated by the lack of decent lapel pins available for events and clubs. So, taking matters into his own hands, he began The Pin People, a company that has grown into one of the largest pin-making companies in the world. Since that time, he has made the pins for thousands of curling clubs, championships—including most national and international events—and in 1988, the Olympics. There are not many curling pins today that don't come from Artiss's company. And it's expanded into pin-making for just about every type of event or occasion—sporting or otherwise—imaginable. Each year, it produces hundreds of thousands of pins. For many years, the company was the official pin-maker for the Olympic Games.

In addition to his pin-making business, Artiss served as chairman of the 1973 World Championship as well as the 1976 Brier. For his efforts, Artiss was inducted into the Canadian Curling Hall of Fame in 2006.

THE CURLING TERMINATOR

Eisschiessen is a popular game in Austria and is still played to this day. It is very similar to curling except that it uses "eisstocks," which resemble bowling pins stuck on a Frisbee instead of stones. In many places around the world, Eisschiessen is played on curling rinks.

While it doesn't take a great deal of muscle to get the eisstocks down the ice, one of Austria's past national champions of the sport is Arnold Schwarzenegger's father.

THE RICHARDSONS

Just as Gordie Howe is to hockey and Babe Ruth is to baseball, the Richardsons are to curling. A Saskatchewan family of two brothers—Ernie and Garnet (known as Sam)—and two cousins, Arnold and Wes, they were the first team to win four Brier titles. They accomplished this remarkable feat in just five appearances. A few notes about the famed family:

- The four are the sons of three brothers and, just to confuse matters, two of them married sisters. Sam and Ernie are brothers, while Arnold and Wes are cousins.
- Sam and Ernie attended the 1955 Brier in Regina and decided then and there that they wanted to play in that event. "I don't think you'll make it. I think you should have started earlier if you wanted to get into that," their mother told the two boys in their early 20s.
- The Richardsons are the only curling team to appear on the cover of *Maclean's* magazine.
- By 1960, the Richardsons were so popular, Ernie gave his name to a line of curling accessories—sweaters, brooms, boots... even socks. The team ended up making about $100,000 from the sale of these items.
- The team lost just seven games in five Brier appearances.

- A lobster supper may have prevented the team from winning a fifth Brier. In 1964 in Charlottetown, the night before the final draw, the team attended a lobster dinner at the home of a friend, and the seafood didn't sit well in the stomachs of the Prairie boys. None slept well that night and they came out flat, losing their last game and any chance of a fifth title.

- Although there were rumours of dissension on the team, Wes Richardson didn't play with the team when it won its record fourth Brier in 1963 because of a bad back. His replacement that year was Mel Perry.

- After winning the Canadian title in 1959 and '60, the Richardsons lost out in 1962, never making it past the Regina city playdowns.

- In 1960, before there were playoffs, the Richardsons secured the title with one draw left to play, a draw in which they had a bye. When the award ceremonies started, the four players walked down the ice holding hands in what fans thought was a show of team solidarity. In truth, they celebrated heartily during their bye and were trying to keep each other from falling down.

- The team won the first World Curling Championship by defeating a team of Scots in the Scotch Cup. They followed up with three more world championship wins.

- In 1960, the City of Regina planned a massive civic reception for the team but was unsure when they were to arrive home from Scotland and a second Scotch Cup victory. When they finally received word of the date, it was too early, and so despite having been away for three weeks, the Richardsons were told to spend three extra days in Toronto while the reception was organized.
- The Richardsons were just the second team from Saskatchewan to win the Brier, after Garnet Campbell in 1955.
- Despite several tries, the team was never able to make it back to the Brier, and they disbanded in 1968.

A WOMAN'S PLACE

Shannon Kleibrink may be best known as the skip of Canada's team at the 2006 Olympics, but she holds another distinction of note: she is the only woman to skip a team to the Canadian Mixed championship.

MULTI-TALENTED

Pierre Charette of Quebec is the only player to compete in a Brier at all four positions. In 1989 and '93, he skipped Quebec's entry. In 1996 he played lead; a year later, second; and a year after that he was third.

THE SHOT

It's been called the greatest shot in the history of the Brier. It is certainly one of the most dramatic—it's a tenth-end, last-rock double takeout made by Northern Ontario's Al Hackner at the 1985 Brier to score two points and tie up the game against Pat Ryan of Alberta. Hackner went on to win in one of the most stunning comebacks in the event's history. Some background on what has come to be known as The Shot:

- Ryan finished the round robin at 11–0, while Hackner was 7–4.
- Ryan's team hadn't had an end stolen on them all week and gave up just one two-ender.
- When Ryan played his last shot, he thought he'd made it impossible for Hackner to score two, and therefore won the Brier. He came down the ice with his broom over his head in a premature celebration. Others thought he'd won too as photographers jumped all over the ice even though Hackner's last rock was still to come. It took almost 10 minutes to restore order to allow Hackner to play his shot.
- Neither Hackner nor his third, Rick Lang, saw Ryan's mini-celebration as they were busy lining up the final shot.
- When Ryan got down to the other end, he saw he'd left Hackner a shot. "From my perspective [at the other end], it looked as

thought I had made the shot," Ryan said later. "But actually I hadn't—I'd lined it up."

- Hackner's team had played three shots down the same path as his final rock that end, so he knew the ice.

- After he made the shot, the fans in the arena went crazy. But Hackner slid stone-faced down the ice, and as he passed Ryan said one word: "Sorry."

- When Hackner arrived beside Lang at the other end, Lang congratulated his skip, but also pointed out another problem: "Nice shot, skipper," he said. "Now how the hell are we going to steal one." The shot only tied the game, sending it to an extra end.

- In the extra end, Alberta second Gord Trenchie missed both shots, and when Ryan came to throw his last rock, he needed to draw to a piece of the four-foot. His rock came into the rings, and Hackner swept it back enough that it gave them a single point—and the Brier crown to Northern Ontario.

- Lang normally swept the opposition rocks when they came into the house, but for some reason, on this occasion, as Ryan's stone neared the tee line, he didn't move, and Hackner jumped in at the last second to sweep it back.

- Hackner believes that if Ryan played more aggressively early in that final game, he would have won the game easily.

- Although happy at winning, Lang felt remorseful at defeating Ryan, who was the best team that week. "There was almost a feeling of guilt," Lang admitted. "We know how Ryan's team felt because it happened to us [in 1981]. It really took something away from winning."

WORLD CHAIR

In 2002, the World Curling Federation sanctioned the first World Wheelchair Curling Championship. Although there were not a lot of competitors at first, the discipline has grown over the years, and made its first appearance at the Paralympics in 2006.

World Wheelchair Curling Champions

2002	Switzerland
2003	No competition
2004	Scotland
2005	Scotland
2006	no event due to Paralympics (Canada)
2007	Norway
2008	Norway

Curling Fact
The oldest sporting club in North America is the Royal Montreal Curling Club, founded in 1807.

STATS

The best teams don't always win the championship. At least not when it comes to statistics. The Canadian Curling Association has kept individual and team shooting percentages at its national championships since 1982, and often times, the team with the best average isn't the champion.

Here's a look at the all-time top team shooting percentages and the teams' final positions:

Women

%	Team	Year	Finish
85	Canada (Jones)	2002	First
83	Saskatchewan (Betker)	2007	Second
83	Saskatchewan (Lawton)	2005	Fourth
83	Ontario (Hanna)	2005	Second
83	Alberta (King)	2002	Tied fifth
83	Ontario (Middaugh)	2002	Third
83	Saskatchewan (Schmirler)	1997	First
83	Canada (Peterson)	1995	Third
83	Canada (Peterson)	1994	First

Men

%	Team	Year	Finish
89	Ontario (Middaugh)	2001	Third
88	Alberta (Ferbey)	2004	Second
88	Ontario (Werenich)	1990	First
87	Alberta (Martin)	2007	Fourth
87	Alberta (Ferbey)	2003	First
87	N.B. (Howard)	2003	Fourth
87	Manitoba (Stoughton)	2000	Second
87	Ontario (Howard)	1993	First
86	Ontario (Howard)	2006	Second
86	Alberta (Ferbey)	2005	First
86	New Brunswick (Howard)	2004	Fifth
86	Ontario (Corner)	2000	Fifth
86	Quebec (Roberge)	2000	Third
86	Ontario (Middaugh)	1998	First

LONG-DISTANCE CURLING

Some teams will do anything for a shot at the Brier, but Bob Chilton and his rink, from the End of the Rail Curling Club, might take top prize if there was one for perseverance. The team played out of a club in Moose Factory, Ontario, a native reserve on an island across from Moosonee on the southern tip of James Bay. To reach their club to practise, the team travelled three miles across the Moose River by snowmobile—which meant they had to wait until mid-December for the freeze-up.

In 1987–88, to reach their zone playdowns, the rink had to fly to Timmins (about 250 miles as the crow flies), but because of a snowstorm, the plane almost didn't take off. Timmins was only the first stop. After arriving there, the team had to drive three and a half hours through the blizzard to Kapuskasing, arriving just minutes before their first game. They won their zone that year, advanced through the association level, and made it as far as the provincial championship before losing.

RYAN'S EXPRESS

One of the most dominant curlers of his era, Pat Ryan had a lengthy and distinguished career on the ice. A three-time Canadian champion, he continues to compete to this day. Some notes about Ryan:

- He is one of just two curlers to play in Briers in four different decades ('70s, '80s, '90s, and '00s). The other is Peter Hollett of Newfoundland and Labrador.
- In 1985, thinking he had won the Brier after his last shot, Ryan came down the ice with his broom in the air in celebration. However, Northern Ontario's Al Hackner played what is often regarded as the most dramatic last shot in Brier history to tie the game and then beat Ryan in an extra end.
- He won back-to-back Briers in 1988 and '89 on the strength of an extremely defensive style of play, playing a vast majority of takeouts and winning low-scoring games.
- He moved to British Columbia in 1991 and, in 1993, won another Brier playing third for Rick Folk. He became just the second player to win a Brier as skip and then at another position.
- He created and marketed a series of curler trading cards that sold extremely well.
- He has two other national titles to his credit. He won the 2007 Canadian senior and the 1986 Canadian Mixed.
- Ryan's daughter, Lynsay, appeared nude in a calendar to raise awareness and funds for women's curling.

WHAT A CROWD

Brier attendance figures have steadily increased over the years. Here is a look at some notable milestones when it comes to the turnstiles:

First Brier to reach 50,000	Regina, 1955	(51,725)
First Brier to reach 100,000	Brandon, 1982	(106,394)
First Brier to reach 150,000	Saskatoon, 1989	(151,538)
First Brier to reach 200,000	Calgary, 1997	(223,322)
First Brier to reach 225,000	Edmonton, 1999	(242,887)
First Brier to reach 275,000	Edmonton, 2005	(281,985)

Brier opening ceremonies

VERA NICE

Saskatchewan curler Vera Pezer is one of the first stars of women's curling, with four Canadian championships in five years. Pezer has many other accomplishments in curling and her business life that make her one of the most remarkable people to play the roaring game. A few notes on the career of Vera Pezer:

- She learned the game in her hometown of Meskanaw, Saskatchewan, on a two-sheet natural ice club her father maintained.
- She won her first Canadian title in 1969, playing third for Joyce McKee. For the next three titles, she played skip while McKee moved to second.
- After winning three consecutive titles, the team disbanded.
- She holds a Ph.D. in sports psychology and served as sports psychologist for two Canadian Olympic teams.
- She did some work with another Saskatchewan legend, Sandra Schmirler.
- She is currently the chancellor of the University of Saskatchewan.
- She wrote two books on curling: *Smart Curling: Perfect Your Game Through Mental Training* and *The Stone Age: A Social History of Curling in the Prairies*.
- She won two national fastball titles in 1969 and '70 as part of the Saskatoon Imperials, and played in two Canadian Senior Women's Golf Championships.

MONCTON 100

The richest bonspiel in curling history took place in 1990 in Moncton, New Brunswick. The event was created to help celebrate the city's centennial and it pitted 16 top teams playing for $250,000. It is still the most lucrative bonspiel ever held and also one of the most significant in that it was the first to utilize rules that are now standard. Some notes about this legendary bonspiel:

- The field included two women's teams, skipped by Heather Houston and Linda Moore, four European teams, and two from Atlantic Canada. The rest were hand-picked by the organizers from across the country.
- This was the first major event to use a variation of the free-guard zone. The rule stated that leads could not play takeouts on rocks anywhere between the hog line and the tee line. It was a huge hit with the curlers.
- The event was the first to include a separate singles' skills competition for an extra purse. The players in the main event also participated in the challenge, being scored on their ability to play a number of difficult shots. A similar challenge was later added to both the men's and women's Canadian championships.
- It was the first event to use a draw to the button to determine last rock. All four players threw one stone, and the team with the lesser cumulative distance had last rock in the first end.

- The teams were charged an entry fee of $1,000 but received free airfare to Moncton, complimentary hotel rooms and, if they lost all their games, $1,500 in prize money.
- With the new free-guard zone rule in place, most games were high-scoring, close affairs ... except for the final. Ed Lukowich defeated Russ Howard 13–2 to win the Moncton 100. Lukowich earned $100,000 for the victory.

CRAZY FOR CURLING

People called Ken Murphy crazy, and he didn't mind one bit. An enthusiastic curler from Wallaceburg, Ontario, Murphy was known as Crazy Legs for the manner in which he danced—and for what he did on the curling ice. At his annual curling bonspiel at the Sydenham Curling Club, he would slide down a sheet of curling ice perched atop a stone, often waving flags or playing a trombone. At the extreme level, Murphy placed the legs of a ladder on four stones and then scrambled to the top rung, where he sat as the rocks travelled over the ice. He became so famous for his act that he appeared on television and at big curling events. He also ran a famous bonspiel that, at its peak in the late 1980s, had a five-year waiting list.

SPIEL OF A DIFFERENT KIND

Every weekend during the curling season, there are bonspiels of all shapes and sizes held all over the world. Most fall into a couple of broad categories: men's, women's, or mixed; competitive or social; one-day or longer. However, a few almost defy description. Here is a sampling of some rather unusual bonspiels held over the years:

Heavyweight Spiel: organized by legendary promoter Doug Maxwell on behalf of a Toronto delicatessen chain, the total weight of the team members could be no less than 1,000 pounds, and individually, no competitor could weigh less than 225.

Left-Handers Spiel: Every spring at the Oakville Curling Club outside of Toronto, the World Lefthanders Championship is held where southpaws battle it out to become global port-sider champion.

Grits vs. Tories: Back in the 1850s, this annual affair pitted the two sides of the government of the day with the losers required to buy a meal of oysters for the winners.

Summer Spud: Capitalizing on being one of Canada's great summertime playgrounds, folks at the Crapaud Curling Club in Prince Edward Island hold an annual spiel … in August! It includes a lobster feast and 18 holes of golf.

Watson Lake Outdoor Bonspiel: Curling outside in the middle of February in the Yukon Territory might not seem that appealing, but obviously some folks like it. Played on the lake from which the bonspiel takes its name, this is the longest-running outdoor bonspiel in Canada.

THE LONG BRIER ROAD

In Canada, approximately 7,000 curlers enter the play-downs every year that lead to the Brier, the Canadian championship. Of course, at the end of it, only four stand atop the highest step on the podium.

ROCK-SOLID POLITICS

Paul Delorey proved that politics and curling do mix. Delorey represented the Yukon/Northwest Territories at the 1987 Canadian Mixed. He is also the Speaker of the Northwest Territories Legislature.

ROCKIN' RICK

Thunder Bay, Ontario, has produced many great curling champions, but the best may be Rick Lang, the three-time Canadian men's champion who some believe is the best third to have played the game.

Some interesting facts about Lang:

- Ed Werenich calls him the best curler ever to play the game.
- Lang won his first Brier in 1975 playing for Bill Tetley. In 1985, he won his third with Bill's son, Ian, playing second.
- Lang joined forces with skip Al Hackner in 1980 and lost the Canadian final. The very next year, Kerry Burtnyk scored three in the 10th end of the final to beat them 5–4. They finally won the title in 1982 and again in 1985.
- At many events, Lang would bet anyone willing to put up $20 that he could throw a rock down a sheet and drink a beer before the rock arrived at the other end. With the money on the table, Lang would throw a slow draw with a mighty spin cranked on the handle so the stone turned like a 78 rpm record, thereby taking a long time to reach its destination. Lang could also drink a beer quickly.
- On the way home from winning the 1985 World Curling Championships in Germany, a flight attendant, noticing there was a lot of attention being paid to Lang, said to him, "Are you who we think you are?" Lang, thinking they knew him as the

curler, replied, "Yes I am." The flight attendant squealed, "Mr. Jagger, may I have your autograph." Lang bears a striking resemblance to Rolling Stones' lead man Mick Jagger.

- Lang holds the dubious distinction of being the only Canadian curler to lose games at the world championship to both France and Italy.
- Lang's wife, Lorraine, won two Canadian women's championships. Together, they won the Canadian Mixed.
- In 2006, Lang and Hackner joined forces again to win the Canadian Senior Championship.

Curling Quote

"Curling is not a sport. I called my grandmother and told her she could win a gold medal because they have dusting in the Olympics now."

—Former NBA star and now outspoken television commentator
Charles Barkley

CUT SHORT

Curling is an extremely popular sport on television, so much so that networks and curling associations should know better than to mess with those watching. Two examples prove that out:

- In 1987, the CBC showed the semi-final of the Brier between Mark Noseworthy of Newfoundland and British Columbia's Bernie Sparkes. The game went longer than expected, and the network elected to cut away from the curling in favour of the evening news. With five rocks left to play, the coverage left the curling to show the warm-up of a game between the Montreal Canadiens and the Philadelphia Flyers. The CBC switchboard was flooded with phone calls from irate curlers, and a new policy was put in place to allow any curling game to finish, regardless of the time.

- In 2005, the Canadian Curling Association signed a new broadcast agreement with CBC that moved round-robin games away from fan favourite TSN to a subscription channel owned by the CBC called Country Canada. When the first game of the Canadian Women's Championship aired and curling fans were unable to find it on TSN, the Canadian Curling Association's head office received such an onslaught of phone calls, it shut down its phone line. A year later, under much pressure, the round-robin games returned to TSN.

THE ICEMAN CURLETH

Al Hackner was known in curling circles as "The Iceman" for the cool, emotionless demeanour he exhibited on the ice, even in tense situations. The curler from Thunder Bay, Ontario, won two Canadian and world championships and a great many cashspiels over his career. He is also credited with throwing the most dramatic shot in Brier history—a nearly impossible 10th-end double takeout that led to his second Canadian championship. And he never let a party stand in the way of a good bonspiel. Here are some notes about Al Hackner:

- He named his dog Tankard, after the trophy awarded to the Canadian champions.
- He played second in the 1976 Canadian mixed championship for Alberta, while living in Edmonton.
- He realized near the end of his career that he may have enjoyed himself a little too much during his heyday. "I'll be the first to admit I probably wasn't disciplined enough," he said in *Curling: The History, The Players, The Game* by Warren Hansen. "When I played seriously, we'd always have beer and the stereo going."
- After winning his first world championship, Hackner was voted the second most recognizable person in his home town of Thunder Bay. The mayor was first.

- At the 1980 Brier, Hackner and his team decided they wanted to see if Paul Gowsell, who represented Alberta and was the game's leading money winner, was as wild a party animal as the stories made him out to be. For the first few days, Hackner and his front end of Bruce Kennedy and Bob Nicol went to Gowsell's room every night to drink beer. On the fourth night, they arrived to find the door locked, and claimed victory in the party wars.
- Hackner started curling on natural ice in Nipigon, Ontario.
- He worked for more than 30 years for CN, serving as a switcher, trainman, and conductor.

MARILYN BODOGH

One of the most colourful figures in women's curling is Marilyn Bodogh, a two-time World Curling champion from St. Catharines, Ontario. Bodogh won titles in 1986 and '96, and was an active player on the competitive circuit for close to 20 years. A few notes about this lively lady:

- She made her first appearance at the Canadian championship playing third for her sister, Christine Bodogh. When she won her first world championship, Christine (Jurgenson) played second.
- She spent several years as a commentator on broadcasts of World Curling Tour events on Rogers Sportsnet.
- In 2006, she ran for the position of mayor of St. Catharines, finishing third out of eight candidates.
- Through marriage (when she was known as Marilyn Darte), she helped operate a family-owned funeral home, leading the *Globe and Mail* to start a story on her with the following line: "The only things certain in Marilyn Darte's life are death and curling."
- In 1987, as defending champion, Bodogh was in Lethbridge, Alberta, to promote that year's national championship. She attended a press conference at a Lethbridge curling club, and when a photographer suggested going onto the ice to take

some pictures, Bodogh walked out, interrupted a game being played by some seniors, put a rock on the button, and then, despite wearing a skirt, did a cartwheel behind the rock. The photographer got his shot.

- Bodogh almost always wore a kilt when playing. As well, she wore green bloomers underneath.
- In 2008, she played in the Ontario senior championships for the first time, finishing second.
- Bodogh works as a motivational speaker.

HOG WILD

Prior to the introduction of the electronic hog line sensor, officials called violations on curlers who slid over the line without releasing the stone. The curlers who were called for the violations almost always disagreed, and some did so vehemently. And the more significant the event, the more they disagreed. Here are two of the most controversial hog line decisions:

• At the 2001 World Curling Championships in Lausanne, Switzerland, Canadian skip Randy Ferbey was playing the semi-final against Switzerland's Andreas Schwaller. Ferbey was called three times for hog line violations, with the penalty being the removal of his rock. The official was Swiss, and for some unusual reason, that week, most of the violations came against the opponents of the Swiss team. Canada lost the game 6–5 to Switzerland, and Ferbey made his mark by chewing out the official after the third pull. Television replays show Ferbey clearly releasing the stone before the hog line. "It's unfortunate that something like that got to dictate the way of the game going," Ferbey said. "All week long I had one hog line call and all of a sudden I have three. I definitely question how they came to determine how I was over the hog line."

• In the semi-final of the 1987 Ontario championships, Paul Savage played Russ Howard. In the eighth end of a close game, Savage played a takeout for two points, but before the stones were kicked off, an official came out and called Savage for a hog line violation. Instead of Savage scoring two, Howard took one and went on to win the game. Savage was livid for a number of reasons. First, sliding over the hog line on a takeout was nearly impossible, and Savage didn't slide very long at the best of times. Second, instead of the necessary two hog line officials—one on either side of the sheet—there was only one. Third, in his many years of curling, Savage had never been called for a hog line violation. Even Howard said after the game he was surprised the rock was pulled.

Curling Fact

At the first Brier, there was only one team from Western Canada, Ossie Barkwell's rink from Yellowgras , Saskatchewan . The foursome earned the invitation by winning the Manitoba bonspiel that year, and a week after that victory they left for Toronto, taking their own rocks along with them.

SINGULARLY REWARDING

Although curling is a team game, each year, many of the major championships hand out individual awards for various achievements. Here is a look at the awards and the criteria for winning:

Event/Association	Award	Given For
World Curling Championship	Colin Campbell Award	Presented to the male curler who best displays the ideals of sportsmanship and skill during the event
World Curling Championship	Frances Brodie Award	Presented to the female curler who is judged to exemplify the best sportsmanship
World Curling Federation	Elmer Freytag Award	Presented to an individual who has shown sportsmanship, character, and leadership either as a competitor or builder
Tim Hortons Brier	Ross Harstone Award	Awarded to the player who exhibits high ideals of good sportsmanship, observance of the rules, exemplary conduct, and curling ability
Tim Hortons Brier	Hec Gervais Award	Presented to the curler judged the most valuable during the Brier
Scotties Tournament of Hearts	Marj Mitchell Award	Presented to the curler who best exemplifies the spirit of curling
Scotties Tournament of Hearts	Sandra Schmirler Award	Presented to the curlers judged the most valuable during the Scotties
U.S. National Championship	Ann Brown Award	Presented to one male and one female recipient judged by their peers to exemplify the best in sportsmanship

PHOTO CREDITS

Page 6: *Ontario Curling Report*

Page 17: Denis Drever / *Ontario Curling Report*

Page 27: Powell Photo / Estate of Doug Maxwell

Page 31: H.C. Fortier Limited / Estate of Doug Maxwell

Page 32: Courtesy Marco Ferraro

Page 40: *Ontario Curling Report*

Page 41: *Ontario Curling Report*

Page 45: Estate of Doug Maxwell

Page 52: Courtesy John Kawaja

Page 56: Estate of Doug Maxwell

Page 62: Michael Burns Photography Ltd. / *Ontario Curling Report*

Page 70: Office du Tourisme Megève / Estate of Doug Maxwell

Page 79: L.H. Shaw, *The Leader-Post* / Estate of Doug Maxwell

Page 87: *Ontario Curling Report*

Page 97: Estate of Doug Maxwell

Page 106: Chiang / *Ontario Curling Report*

Page 112: Courtesy Hans Frauenlob

Page 118: Estate of Doug Maxwell

Page 120: Turofsky, Alexandra Studio / Estate of Doug Maxwell

Page 124: Estate of Doug Maxwell

Page 140: Courtesy TSN

Page 153: *Ontario Curling Report*

Page 162: *Ontario Curling Report*

Page 169: *Kitchener-Waterloo Record* / Estate of Doug Maxwell

Page 178: *Ontario Curling Report*

Page 188: Courtesy TSN

Page 190: *Ontario Curling Report*

INDEX

Bekkeluns, Hans, 18
Belcourt, Tim, 101, 102
Bemidji Curling Club, 4
Beveridge, Corie, 13
Bible, 137
blue hone granite, 160
blue trefor granite, 160
Bobcaygeon Curling Club,
    36–37
Bodogh [Jurgenon],
    Christine, 189
Bodogh, Marilyn, 189–
    90, *190* (*See also* Darte,
    Marilyn)
Boston Arena, 16
boxing, 34
Bradbeen, Dick, 146, 147
Brandon Sun, 166
Braunstein, Terry, 97
Brier: 2, 4, 25, 80, 81, 124,
    125, 147, 151, 178, 183;
    (1927) 22, 111, 120, 125,
    136, 151; (1929) 98;
    (1930) 20; (1931) 151;
    (1932) 20; (1934) 98;
    (1936) 79, 122; (1938)
    98; (1940) 21, 98; (1949)
    79; (1946) 25; (1947) 98,
    122; (1949) 27, 98; (1951)
    98, 109; (1952) 98; (1954)
79, 117, 118; (1955) 98,
168, 170, 178; (1956) 31,
119; (1957) 61, 98, 118;
(1959) 169; (1960) 105,
169; (1962) 155, 166,
169; (1963) 169; (1964)
169; (1965) 97; (1966)
137; (1967) 97; (1969)
98; (1970) 64, 97; (1970)
132; (1971) 25, 60, 97,
118; (1972) 57, 97; (1973)
161; (1974) 15, 29; (1975)
60, 184; (1976) 109, 167;
(1978) 97; (1979) 97;
(1980) 62, 80, 148, 184,
188; (1981) 172; (1982) 57,
62, 97, 178, 184; (1983),
14, 94, 97; (1984) 53, 94;
(1985) 57, 62, 65, 97, 171–
72, 177, 184; (1986) 97;
(1987) 186; (1988) 84, 98,
177; (1989) 24, 84, 101,
170, 177, 178; (1990) 97;
(1990) 51; (1991) 24, 97,
177; (1993) 103, 170, 177;
(1996) 170; (1997) 97, 116,
178; (1999) 178; (2000)
103; (2001) 93, 133–34;
(2003) 98; (2004) 64–65;
(2005) 25, 178; (2007) 13,

Garza, Josele, 68
Gellard, Kim, 13
Gemmell, Maymar, 17
gender battles. *See* battle of
the sexes
Germany, 3, 14, 184
Gerster, Stan, 72
Gervais, Hec, 15, 34, 64, 155
Globe and Mail, 189
golf, 23, 104, 111, 138, 141,
179, 183
Governor-General's Club,
129
Governor-General's trophy,
129
Gowanlock, Ab, 98
Gowsell, Paul, 44, 188
Graham, Sandy, 13
Grand Banks (NF), 144
Grand Caledonian Curling
Club, 7
Grand Match (1848), 139
"Grand Match at Linlithgow
Loch" (painting), 139
Grand National Curling Club,
125
Grand Slam of Curling, 85
Granite Club (Toronto), 2
Granite Curling Club, 22–23
granite, types of, 160–61

Gray, Glenn, 117
Great Britain, 76, 108, 124,
150
Gretzky, Wayne, 71
grey trefor (granite), 160
Grits vs. Tories spiel, 182
Gross, Paul, 38
Grossart, Jack, 63, 164
Grossart Super Brush, 63
Guinness Book of World Records,
20, 163
Gushue, Brad, 13, 54, 78,
110

Hackner, Al ("The Iceman"),
65, 97, 100, 171–72, 177,
184, 187–88
hacks, 32–33, 135
Haig, Senator Jack, 123
Halifax, 117, 120, 136, 145,
150
halls of fame. *See* Canadian
Curling Hall of Fame; U.S.
Curling Hall of Fame
Haluptzok, Mark, 67
Hamilton (ON), 24, 71, 91,
121
Hamilton Spectator, 121
Hamilton-Temple-
Blackwood, Frederick. *See*

National Basketball Association (NBA), 185

National Basketball League, 16

National Hockey League (NHL), 16, 71

National Post, 71

Nashville Curling Club, 72

Neale, Harry, 120

Nedohin, Dave, 57, 84, 85

Nedohin, Heather, 57

Neff, Aubrey, 81–82

New Brunswick, 61, 103, 175

New York, 37

New York City, 54

Newfoundland/Labrador, 60, 109–10, 177, 186

Newton, Laurie, 29

nicknames, 97

Nichols, Bob, 148

Nicol, Bob, 188

Nokia (sponsor), 126

Northcott, Ron, 88, 98

Northern Ontario, 65, 82, 90, 92, 111, 117, 151, 171–72, 177

Northwest Territories, 183

Norway, 18, 173

Noseworthy, Mark, 186

occupations, 111

Odishaw, Grant, 100

Office Depot, 143–44

Okelsrud, Hans, 18

Oland, Sid, 80

older players, 164

Olson, Elias Bjarni ("Ole"), 135

Olympic Stadium (Montreal), 32

Olympics, 5, 57, 58, 79, 96, 179: (1924) 23, 108; (1932) 156; (1975) 28; (1987) 52; (1988) 50, 167; (1992) 50, 132–33, 164; (1998) 5, 14, 68, 108; (2001) 65; (2002) 76, 78, 102, 113, 138, 143; (2006), 67, 78, 110, 113, 164, 170; (2010) 72

Ontario, 52, 62, 94, 101, 109–10, 119, 132, 158, 174, 175

Ontario Curling Association, 6, 52, 123, 156

Ontario Curling Report, 15, 146–47

Ontario double-rink competition, 129

Ontario Senior Championship, 190

Turner Curling Museum,
136–37
Turner, Don, 136, 137
Turner, Elva, 136, 137
Twist, 1

United States Men's
Championship, 67
United States Curling
Association, 125
United States Curling
Championship, 16
United States Women's
Curling Association, 130
University of Minnesota, 23
University of Saskatchewan,
179
U.S. Curling Hall of Fame,
3, 50
U.S. National Championship,
193
U.S. Olympic Committee,
67, 68
U.S. Olympic team, 144
USA Today, 93
Usackis, John, 94
Utica Curling Club, 37
Uusipaavalniemi, Maskku,
111, 112

Vacaville (CA), 55
Vancouver Fire Department,
81
Veale, Fred, 47, 48
Victoria (BC), 53, 118
Vierumaki (Finland), 165
Villeneuve, Camille, 163
visible minority players, 116
vision-impaired players, 82,
91, 162

Walchuk, Don, 100
Wales, 106, 160
walkie-talkies, 101–2
Walsh, Billy, 98, 119
Ward, Phil, 164
warming up, 29–30
Watkins, Jack, 164
Watson, Grant, 27, 79, 122
Watson, Ken, 27
Watson, Harry, 120
Watson, Ken ("Mr. Curling"),
26–27, 79, 88, 98, 122
Watson Lake Outdoor
Bonspiel, 183
Waterman, Grant, 80
Welsh, Jimmy, 98, 122
Welsh, Robin, 29–30, 55
Wendorf, Keith, 17
Werenich, Ed, 14, 51–53,

CURLING, ETCETERA

215